THE GREENHAVEN PRESS
Literary Companion
TO AMERICAN LITERATURE

READINGS ON

THE CRUCIBLE

David Bender, *Publisher*
Bruno Leone, *Executive Editor*
Bonnie Szumski, *Series Editor*
Thomas Siebold, *Book Editor*

Greenhaven Press, San Diego, CA

1654 7281
A

Every effort has been made to trace the owners of copyrighted material. The articles in this volume may have been edited for content, length, and/or reading level. The titles have been changed to enhance the editorial purpose. Those interested in locating the original source will find the complete citation on the first page of each article.

Library of Congress Cataloging-in-Publication Data

Readings on The Crucible / Thomas Siebold, book editor.
        p.   cm. — (The Greenhaven Press literary
companion to American literature.)
     Includes bibliographical references and index.
     ISBN 1-56510-848-5 (pbk. : alk. paper). —
ISBN 1-56510-849-3 (lib. bdg. : alk. paper)
     1. Miller, Arthur, 1915–   Crucible. 2. Historical
drama, American—History and criticism. 3. Salem
(Mass.)—In literature. 4. Witchcraft in literature.
I. Siebold, Thomas. II. Series.
PS3525. I5156C738   1999
812'.52—dc21   98-21205
                                                                    CIP

Cover photo: © Hulton Getty/Tony Stone Images

Copyright ©1999 by Greenhaven Press, Inc.
PO Box 289009
San Diego, CA 92198-9009
Printed in the U.S.A.

" Theater should be speaking to its moment, but it ought to keep alive the past or you won't have any future. "

Arthur Miller

CONTENTS

Chapter 1: Historical Background of *The Crucible*

The Crucible compares the Salem witchcraft trails of 1692
to the Communist hunt of Senator Joseph McCarthy in the
1950s. But the Salem events go beyond the political madness of McCarthyism to reveal the need of a repressive society to publicly articulate its communal guilt.

Arthur Miller's investigation of Salem's history ultimately led
to two central dramatic themes: Guilt can destroy personality
and evil can consume otherwise normal individuals.

The Crucible is an artistic work that explores the meaning
of America's past as it relates to the present. Based on historical records, *The Crucible* presents the audience with a
dramatic cultural study.

Despite popular audience support, *The Crucible* was often
criticized for lacking in-depth characterization, intellectual
complexity, and a clear, meaningful message. Some reviewers charged Miller with creating nothing more than a vague,
self-righteous cry of liberal dissent built on very few specific, identifiable beliefs.

Chapter 2: Characterization and Themes in *The Crucible*

The leading players in *The Crucible* are complex, intriguing, and rich in absorbing character traits. The main character, John Proctor, is a tragic hero who is transformed by self-awareness and understanding.

FOREWORD

*"'Tis the good reader that
makes the good book."*

Ralph Waldo Emerson

The story's bare facts are simple: The captain, an old and scarred seafarer, walks with a peg leg made of whale ivory. He relentlessly drives his crew to hunt the world's oceans for the great white whale that crippled him. After a long search, the ship encounters the whale and a fierce battle ensues. Finally the captain drives his harpoon into the whale, but the harpoon line catches the captain about the neck and drags him to his death.

A simple story, a straightforward plot—yet, since the 1851 publication of Herman Melville's *Moby-Dick*, readers and critics have found many meanings in the struggle between Captain Ahab and the whale. To some, the novel is a cautionary tale that depicts how Ahab's obsession with revenge leads to his insanity and death. Others believe that the whale represents the unknowable secrets of the universe and that Ahab is a tragic hero who dares to challenge fate by attempting to discover this knowledge. Perhaps Melville intended Ahab as a criticism of Americans' tendency to become involved in well-intentioned but irrational causes. Or did Melville model Ahab after himself, letting his fictional character express his anger at what he perceived as a cruel and distant god?

Although literary critics disagree over the meaning of *Moby-Dick*, readers do not need to choose one particular interpretation in order to gain an understanding of Melville's novel. Instead, by examining various analyses, they can gain numerous insights into the issues that lie under the surface of the basic plot. Studying the writings of literary critics can also aid readers in making their own assessments of *Moby-Dick* and other literary works and in developing analytical thinking skills.

The Greenhaven Literary Companion Series was created with these goals in mind. Designed for young adults, this unique anthology series provides an engaging and comprehensive introduction to literary analysis and criticism. The essays included in the Literary Companion Series are chosen for their accessibility to a young adult audience and are expertly edited in consideration of both the reading and comprehension levels of this audience. In addition, each essay is introduced by a concise summation that presents the contributing writer's main themes and insights. Every anthology in the Literary Companion Series contains a varied selection of critical essays that cover a wide time span and express diverse views. Wherever possible, primary sources are represented through excerpts from authors' notebooks, letters, and journals and through contemporary criticism.

Each title in the Literary Companion Series pays careful consideration to the historical context of the particular author or literary work. In-depth biographies and detailed chronologies reveal important aspects of authors' lives and emphasize the historical events and social milieu that influenced their writings. To facilitate further research, every anthology includes primary and secondary source bibliographies of articles and/or books selected for their suitability for young adults. These engaging features make the Greenhaven Literary Companion series ideal for introducing students to literary analysis in the classroom or as a library resource for young adults researching the world's great authors and literature.

Exceptional in its focus on young adults, the Greenhaven Literary Companion Series strives to present literary criticism in a compelling and accessible format. Every title in the series is intended to spark readers' interest in leading American and world authors, to help them broaden their understanding of literature, and to encourage them to formulate their own analyses of the literary works that they read. It is the editors' hope that young adult readers will find these anthologies to be true companions in their study of literature.

INTRODUCTION

Readings on The Crucible is designed to help students gain a greater appreciation of one of Arthur Miller's most widely produced plays. The carefully edited collection provides an overview of the play's themes, characterization, structure, philosophy, and impact on American theater. Each essay is readable, manageable in length, and focused on concepts suitable for a beginning exploration of literary criticism. Additionally, this diverse overview of *The Crucible* presents readers with a wealth of material for writing reports, designing oral presentations, and enriching their understanding of drama as art.

The Crucible, first staged in 1953, presents an easily recognizable parallel between Senator Joseph McCarthy's attempt to expose Communists living in postwar America and the Salem witch trials of 1692. With the dramatic alignment of these two episodes, the playwright explores a wide range of social themes: the abuse of power, the debilitating effects of fear, the presence of evil, and the struggle of individual conscience against authority. Although the play filled theaters with appreciative audiences, critics were mixed, often criticizing the play as limited in scope and character development. Miller maintained that *The Crucible* is much more than a topical drama, however, explaining that it is a tragedy built on universal ideas that transcend specific historical events.

The critical essays in *Readings on* The Crucible will help readers comprehend the meaning of the play, discover new methods of evaluating it, and appreciate its dramatic structure. Critical interpretations expose readers to a meaningful vocabulary for approaching fundamental literary questions about the playwright's themes, characters, philosophy, and language. The readings also provide an important framework for understanding Miller's stature as a writer, the historical setting in which he wrote, and his place in the evolution of American theater.

In addition to the essays, *Readings on* The Crucible provides other pertinent material about Arthur Miller. The biographical sketch offers readers background on the author's life and influences on his work. The chronology provides a useful overview of Miller's works and places them in a historical time frame. The bibliography identifies valuable resources for students who want to complete further research.

It is important to understand that though the particulars of the McCarthy hearings fade with time, *The Crucible* remains a powerful play that has a stunning effect on readers and audiences. In short, it has endured as an important drama on its own merits apart from any link to a specific historical event. When John Proctor refuses to accept the intolerable conditions of his confession, he asks, "How may I live without my name? I have given you my soul; leave me my name!" This climactic moment in the drama strikes at the core of the human condition. Universally, human beings must struggle to maintain their identity and their personal code of morality against the forces and pressures of society. Proctor's struggle for self-discovery resonates across time, nationalities, and historical events.

ARTHUR MILLER: A BIOGRAPHY

The major turning point in Arthur Miller's career occurred when his most critically celebrated play, *Death of a Salesman*, opened on Broadway in February 1949. The production of *Death of a Salesman* transformed Miller's life. The play won the Pulitzer Prize, the Antoinette Perry (Tony) Award, and the Drama Critics' Circle Award. Its success brought Miller fame, critical praise, and substantial wealth. Heralded as one of America's most promising young playwrights, Miller secured his fame after more than ten years of artistic struggle.

Few artists achieve their goals as substantially as Arthur Miller did. But despite his success, Miller continues to question his achievements. His concern for the common man and his distrust of society's institutions often make him feel guilty and uncomfortable with his celebrity. He fears that he will no longer be able to write about the poor when he himself is rich, or that perhaps the trappings of fame will separate him from the essential feelings and insights that generated a play like *Death of a Salesman*. In his autobiography, *Timebends: A Life*, Miller writes, "I was not the first to experience the guilt of success (which, incidentally, was reinforced by leftist egalitarian convictions), and though I suspected the truth, I was unable to do much about it." For Arthur Miller, the struggle to write is a struggle to learn about himself, understand his role as a writer in society, and maintain his idealism, integrity, and political views against popular opinion and criticism.

MILLER'S CHILDHOOD

Born on October 17, 1915, in New York City, Arthur Asher Miller grew up in a middle-class household on 112th Street in Manhattan with his older brother, Kermit, younger sister, Joan, and parents, Isidore and Augusta Miller. His father, an Austrian immigrant, was, for most of Arthur's youth, a successful manufacturer of ladies' coats. Isidore, like many practical-minded immigrant Jews, entered the garment business when he came

13

to New York City in the late 1800s. Arthur's mother, a school-teacher before she married Isidore, was a conscientious parent who taught her children the customs and heritage of Judaism. Augusta was an avid reader who, according to Miller, could begin a book in the afternoon, finish it by midnight, and recall its details years later. Since no one in the family but Augusta was a reader, she hired a Columbia University student for two dollars a week to discuss novels with her. Augusta was a bright, sensitive woman who was pressed by Miller's grandfathers into marriage within months of graduating with honors from high school. When she told her children the story of her arranged marriage, Miller remembers that her look would suddenly "blacken as she clenched her jaws in anger. 'Like a cow!' she would mutter." In *Timebends: A Life*, Miller suggests that his mother was a "woman haunted by a world she could not reach out to, by books she would not get to read, concerts she would not get to attend, and above all, interesting people she'd never get to meet."

Arthur lived a comfortable middle-class life until age fourteen. It was at this time, in the early stages of the Great Depression, that the family's garment business failed. The loss of the business in 1928 put a great strain on the Millers: Isidore became depressed, both Kermit and Arthur had to take jobs, and the family was forced to move out of their house. As an adolescent, Arthur was deeply disappointed by his father's inability to cope with the loss: "My father simply went more deeply silent, and his naps grew longer, and his mouth seemed to dry up. I could not avoid awareness of my mother's anger at his waning powers." Arthur was also disillusioned with the economic system that put his family in their new predicament; he grew suspicious of the powers that controlled the wealth and the social machinery of society. Later Miller wrote that the depression made him aware that life was often a struggle against powerful social forces outside of the family.

With the loss of their business, the Millers moved to Brooklyn to be near relatives. Arthur attended James Madison High School, where he was actively involved in football and other sports, not unlike Biff Loman in *Death of a Salesman*. Miller focused on staying in good physical shape and improving his athletic skills, not his studies. His friends were athletes, not intellectuals.

After high school, Miller applied to the University of Michigan, but was rejected because his grades were too low.

To earn money, he took odd jobs, including a brief stint in the garment business doing various low-level tasks. It was here that he witnessed firsthand how salesmen were often brusquely dismissed or ordered about by insensitive buyers and employers. Later, of course, Miller would create the most famous salesman in literature, Willy Loman. In 1932 Miller began to read simply to occupy his mind between jobs. He read voraciously, particularly Russian writers Fyodor Dostoyevsky and Leo Tolstoy. His discovery of the power of literature sparked his dream of becoming a writer.

MILLER'S COLLEGE YEARS

After several rejected applications, Miller was finally admitted to the University of Michigan in 1934, where he studied journalism, economics, and history. His broad range of study made him skeptical that any one discipline or institution had a monopoly on truth. As a sensitive young college student, Miller began a quest to understand how society changed, how it influenced the individual, and how it could be improved. Miller was attracted to the ideals of socialism—especially its concern for the rights and dignity of the common person. Exhilarated by the prospect of a new social order built on reason, Miller and his fellow student socialists expected "a socialist evolution of the planet" that would bestow a "new and just system." Although his enthusiasm for socialism eventually diminished, many of the liberal political and social ideals he formed in college stayed with him throughout his writing career.

In his junior year, Miller entered a college playwriting contest and, to his surprise, won the first prize of $250. His play *No Villain*, whose characters are modeled on Miller's own family members, deals with the tension within a garment manufacturing family during a bitter labor strike. In *No Villain*, Miller introduces many of the themes and conflicts that dominate his later and more artistic works: the tension between selfishness and humanitarianism, class struggle, conflicts between family members, and the healing bond of family loyalty. Encouraged by the praise of *No Villain*, Miller decided to dedicate himself to writing drama.

Miller graduated from college in 1938 with a degree in English and subsequently supported himself by writing for the Federal Theater Project, a government-sponsored program promoting American writers. While with the project, Miller and fellow Michigan graduate Norman Rosten coauthored *Lis-*

ten My Children, an uninspired comedy. The Federal Theater Project did not last long, however: The recently established House Un-American Activities Committee (HUAC) suspected the program of infiltration by Communists and abolished it. With the project closed, Miller not only lost his twenty-two-dollar weekly salary, he was also introduced to the harsh tactics of HUAC. Sixteen years later, in 1956, Miller encountered HUAC again when the committee suspected him of subversive behavior and subpoenaed him to defend his social and political views.

MILLER'S EARLY WORK

In 1940 Miller married his sweetheart from the University of Michigan, Mary Slattery. Mary, daughter of an insurance salesman, was a bright student who, according to Miller, had more faith in his ability to write than he had himself. Although she was not actively religious, she was reared a Catholic, and at the time of their marriage both sets of parents were concerned about the intermarriage of a Jew and a gentile. Although the religious conflict in their extended family was disconcerting, Miller and his young wife believed that they could rise above the "parochial narrowness of mind, prejudices, racism, and the irrational" that they felt the tension represented. The couple had two children, Robert and Jane. During World War II, Mary worked as a secretary and Arthur, unable to participate in military service because of a nagging football injury, worked on ships in the Brooklyn Navy Yard and wrote radio plays for the Columbia Broadcasting System. Despite the fact that script writing turned out to be rather lucrative (approximately one hundred dollars a script), Miller hated writing for radio; he chafed under the restrictions and limitations imposed by the radio networks and advertisers and became increasingly suspicious of mixing commercialism and the arts. Nevertheless, as the radio scripts demanded crisp writing and tight organization, this work helped the young playwright refine his craft.

Miller received his first theatrical break in 1944 when *The Man Who Had All the Luck* was staged on Broadway. The play explores the roles of fate, luck, success, and failure in one's life. Unfortunately, it was not well received by critics and closed after only six performances. In his autobiography Miller says of this play that "standing at the back of the house during the single performance I could bear to watch, I could blame nobody. All I knew was that the whole thing was a well-meant botch,

like music played on the wrong instruments in a false scale."
Although this play and his other early dramas were unsuc-
cessful, Miller was learning what it took to write a meaningful
play. He developed an ear for dialogue and he learned the craft
of staging dramas, the needs of actors, and the demands of an
audience. Success was not far away.

The Man Who Had All the Luck lost a great deal of money
and Miller, now in debt, felt pressured to write his next project, a novel entitled *Focus*. The story's main character is a
non-Jew named Lawrence Newman who, after he begins to
wear glasses, is mistaken for a Jew. Lawrence is shocked and
outraged when he encounters senseless prejudice and anti-
Semitism. The novel met with moderate success and was published in England, France, Germany, and Italy. As a Jew himself, Miller experienced only limited encounters with
anti-Semitism as a child, but once he began working after high
school he was shocked at the extent and intensity of anti-
Semitism in America. Because of his own anti-Semitic experiences and following revelations of the Holocaust, Miller committed himself to a lifelong fight opposing anti-Semitism.

MILLER'S FIRST DRAMATIC SUCCESS

At age thirty a frustrated Miller, faced with meager respect
and success as a dramatist, decided to give playwriting one
last try. Based on an incidental comment by his wife's mother
about a young girl who turned in her father to the FBI for
manufacturing faulty aircraft parts, Miller began a two-year
task of diligently writing and rewriting the play *All My Sons*.
He had decided that if he was going to fail as a writer, he
would go out with the best possible script. In 1947 this realistic social drama was coproduced by stage and film director
Elia Kazan, who at the time was well known but not yet famous. Kazan helped Miller focus and polish the work.

All My Sons follows a thematic pattern Miller established in
Focus. As the play opens, the audience perceives an atmosphere of normality, a world that is calm, orderly, and peaceful.
This placid world is disrupted as the play progresses and the
characters expose the audience to a world of tension and disillusionment. The intent of the play is to reveal truths about
family, moral decision making, and the role of the individual
in society. Although it received mixed reviews, *All My Sons*
was widely popular with theatergoers and enjoyed a profitable
run of 328 performances. It won the Drama Critics' Circle
Award and provided Miller with the renewed energy and re-

sources to press on in his career. On the heels of its Broadway success, in 1948 *All My Sons* was made into a movie starring Edward G. Robinson and Burt Lancaster.

Reflecting on this period of his life, Miller recalls conflicting emotions. On one hand he was proud of his success, but on the other hand he experienced some awkwardness: "As a success I was occasionally greeted by people on the street with a glazed expression that was pleasant but made me feel unnervingly artificial. My identification with life's failures was being menaced by my fame." Miller's reactions aside, with *All My Sons* his status as a playwright was established.

MILLER'S MASTER DRAMA

With the money he earned from *All My Sons*, Miller bought a modest farm in Roxbury, Connecticut. On a knoll by a woods, Miller built a small cabin to which he could escape and write undisturbed. He notes that while he was building he had but two lines for his next play, based on a salesman he had known when he worked for his father: "Willy!" and "It's all right. I came back." Early one morning, sitting in his completed studio, he started writing and by the morning of the next day he had written half a play, which he called *Inside Your Head*. Producers Walter Fried and Kermit Bloomgarden liked the play immediately and convinced Kazan to direct it. With extensive rewriting, the play opened in February 1949 with a new name—*Death of a Salesman*.

Death of a Salesman premiered in Philadelphia to glowing reviews. In his autobiography, Miller tells of his experience watching the first performance. At play's end the audience did not applaud. Instead, they sat in stunned silence, stood up, put their coats on, and sat down again, not wanting to leave the theater. Some people were crying. Finally, almost as an afterthought, the applause exploded. From Philadelphia the production moved to the Morosco Theater on Broadway where it played to packed houses and overwhelming approval. *Death of a Salesman* ran for 742 performances before it closed on November 18, 1950, having won the Drama Critics' Circle Award and the Pulitzer Prize. On its Broadway premiere, Miller became famous. Again, Miller reveals in his autobiography that he struggled with his success. Reflecting on the glory of the first night after the New York opening, with rave reviews flowing from all the critics, Miller writes, "I had striven all my life to win this night, and it was here, and I was this celebrated man who had amazingly little to do with me, or I with him. . . . My dreams of many years had become too damned real, and the reality was less than the dream."

POLITICAL ACTIVITY AND *THE CRUCIBLE*

In the late 1940s and into the 1950s, the cold war between the Soviet Union and the United States, accompanied by a superpower arms race, created an international mood of suspicion and fear. Political, social, and business leaders were increasingly concerned that communism threatened the American "way of life." This so-called Red Scare often bordered on paranoia. It was a tense era, when federal workers were required to take loyalty oaths to pledge their allegiance to America and the government established loyalty boards to investigate reports of Communist sympathizers. In 1950 Wisconsin senator Joseph McCarthy and the House Un-American Activities Committee, established to uncover subversive infiltration into American life, turned their anti-Communist attention to Hollywood and the intellectual community.

In April 1952, HUAC called Miller's director, Elia Kazan, to testify about Communist activity in the theater and motion-picture business. He was asked to name individuals whom he knew had been members of Communist groups, and Kazan named Miller. Both Kazan and Miller were liberals, who, like many intellectuals and artists, dabbled with leftist ideas and causes. Arthur Miller had attended a few meetings of Communist Writers of New York, had signed a petition that protested the banning of the Communist Party, and had been named in a 1947 issue of the *Daily Worker*, a socialist newspaper. Moreover, during the war years, Miller was intrigued by Marxism and had attended some Marxist study courses. Because of his economic troubles during the depression, Miller felt he had experienced the Marxist struggle of the worker against the employer. In *Timebends: A Life* Miller writes that "the concept of a classless society had a disarming sweetness that called forth the generosity of youth. The true condition of man, it seemed, was the complete opposite of the competitive system that I had assumed was normal, with all its mutual hatreds and conniving." But despite the fact that Miller supported left-wing causes, he was not a Communist Party member or sympathizer. After Kazan, HUAC targeted Miller.

Miller was finally subpoenaed to appear before HUAC in 1956. Unlike his friend Kazan, Miller refused to name names. The committee members were unimpressed with the playwright's explanation of artistic freedom and cited Miller for contempt of Congress. Although Miller was found guilty by an overwhelming vote of 373 to 9, public support for his openness and honesty resulted in a reconsideration of his case. In 1958 the U.S. Court of Appeals for the District of Columbia reversed Miller's conviction, stating that he was not informed adequately of the risks involved in incurring contempt.

Miller's response to this anti-Communist fear, guilt, and hysteria was *The Crucible.* In 1951 Miller read Marion Starkey's book *The Devil in Massachusetts* which details the strange events of the Salem witchcraft trials. Despite the dramatic possibilities of the topic, Miller initially rejected the idea of writing a play on the subject, believing that his own sense of rationality would not allow him to capture the wild irrationality of the events. In his autobiography the playwright writes why he changed his mind, "gradually, over weeks, a living connection between myself and Salem, and between Salem and Washington, was made in my mind—for whatever else they might be, I saw that the hearings in Washington were profoundly and even avowedly ritualistic." Although he had been introduced to the witchcraft trials in his American history class at Michigan, Miller decided to travel to the Historical Society of Salem in order to read firsthand accounts of the phenomenon. Ironically, the day before he left for Salem, Elia Kazan phoned to say that he had agreed to cooperate with HUAC.

At the Salem courthouse Miller studied the town records of 1692. He found that initially the dialect of the interrogations sounded gnarled and he mouthed the words out loud until he "came to love its feel, like burnished wood." In the evenings he walked through the town trying to capture the mood of the period. In his "Introduction" to the *Collected Plays* Miller writes that the lunacy of McCarthyism and the terror of Salem began to merge into a central image that would carry his play, "above all, above all horrors, I saw accepted the notion that conscience was no longer a private matter but one of state administration. I saw men handing conscience to other men and thanking other men for the opportunity of doing so."

The Crucible took Miller almost one year to write. The mood of the country remained tense. According to Miller, the average citizen was willing to accept insanity as routine. In *Timebends: A Life* the playwright exemplifies this mood by recalling the fate of "The Hook," Miller's screenplay about union corruption written in 1951. The head of Columbia Pictures, Harry Cohn, after showing the script to the FBI, wanted Miller to change the gangsters to Communists. When Miller refused, he was chastised by Cohn, "The minute we try to make the script pro-American you pull out." Because of this type of harassment, Miller knew that it would take a great deal of courage for Kermit Bloomgarden to produce *The Crucible* on Broadway. Indeed, the momentum working against Miller was building: In Peoria, Illinois, the American Legion and the Jaycees gained publicity by leading a successful boycott of *Death of a Salesman*, and the Catholic War Veterans had persuaded the army to ban its theatrical groups from staging any Miller play. Nevertheless, *The Crucible* opened on Broadway in 1953 for a decent run of 197 performances. The staging received mixed reviews, but what disappointed the author more than the critical reception of the play was the hostility of the audience. In *Timebends: A Life* Miller writes that "as the theme of the play was revealed, an invisible sheet of ice formed over their heads, thick enough to skate on. In the lobby at the end, people with whom I had some fairly close professional acquaintanceships passed me by as though I were invisible."

As the Red Scare waned, the popularity of *The Crucible* grew. The play had a very successful off-Broadway production in 1954, 1956, and 1965; it was dramatized on television with George C. Scott as John Proctor; and today it is Miller's most frequently produced play, staged every week somewhere in the world for forty-odd years. The Bantam and Penguin editions of *The Crucible* have sold more than 6 million copies. Modern audiences, long past the McCarthy paranoia, enjoy the universal themes that the drama embodies.

In 1996, at age 81, Miller's screenplay of *The Crucible* was released with Daniel Day-Lewis as John Proctor, Joan Allen as Elizabeth, Winona Ryder as Abigail, and Paul Scofield as Judge Danforth. Enjoying the critical success of the movie, Miller looked back on the evolution of the play in an article in the *New Yorker*. He argues that he wrote the play out of desperation, "motivated in some great part by the paralysis that had set in among many liberals who, despite their discomfort with the inquisitors' violations of civil rights, were fearful, and with good reason, of being identified as covert Communists if they should protest too strongly." Although the elderly playwright isn't exactly sure what *The Crucible* is saying to people today, he is confident "that its paranoid center is still pumping out the same darkly attractive warning that it did in the fifties."

MILLER'S LIFE WITH MARILYN MONROE

By 1951 Mary and Arthur's marriage was beginning to deteriorate, perhaps under the demands of a successful writing career or the pressures of celebrity, or perhaps because Elia Kazan had by then introduced Miller to Marilyn Monroe. Miller comments in *Timebends: A Life* that "when we shook hands the shock of her body's motion sped through me, a sensation at odds with her sadness amid all this glamour and technology." At one point Miller characterized the actress as "the golden girl who was like champagne on the screen." Although they had an occasional correspondence, they did not pursue a serious relationship until 1954, when Monroe divorced her husband Joe DiMaggio, one of the most famous baseball players of his era, and moved to New York City.

The next two years were tumultuous for Arthur Miller. In September 1955 two of Miller's one-act plays, *A View from the Bridge* and *A Memory of Two Mondays*, opened at the Coronet Theater in New York to disappointing and discouraging reviews. In June of that year Miller had contracted with the New York City Youth Board to write a screenplay, but when the project was announced reporter Frederick Woltman viciously attacked Miller for his leftist political views in the *New York Herald-Tribune*. The newspaper article and pressure from the paper's management forced the Youth Board to cancel Miller's film project.

In the early months of 1956, Miller divorced Mary Grace Slattery. Soon after the divorce, in the midst of his political battles with HUAC, Miller made the surprise announcement that he and Marilyn Monroe had been secretly married in a Jewish ceremony (only seventeen days after his divorce). Marilyn had just completed filming the movie *Bus Stop*, and, troubled by personal problems, looked forward to a stable life with Miller. The newspapers minutely and voraciously scrutinized the marriage. Marilyn was depicted as a volatile, sexy bombshell and Miller was pictured as a self-sufficient, intellectual writer. The contrast in personalities, the publicity, and the pressures that both were feeling at the time virtually guaranteed that the marriage would suffer.

Throughout the course of their marriage, Miller's writing fell into a slump. Life with Marilyn consumed him; her need for attention, her mood swings, and her reliance on alcohol and drugs required inordinate amounts of Miller's energy. Miller did manage to adapt his short story "The Misfits," which was first published in *Esquire* in 1957, into a screen-play specifically for Marilyn. The movie *The Misfits*, directed by John Huston, was filmed in Nevada with Montgomery Clift, Clark Gable, and Marilyn in the pivotal role of Roslyn. During the filming, Marilyn, haunted by depression and drugs, broke down and required time to recuperate in the hospital. By this time the marriage was close to failure. In his autobiography Miller states that Marilyn, confused about who she was, "wanted everything, but one thing contradicted another; physical admiration threatened to devalue her person, yet she became anxious if her appearance was ignored."

The Misfits was first released in 1961 and met with moderate success. That year Marilyn filed for a Mexican divorce and Miller's mother died. For the next twelve months, Miller kept a low profile, publishing only two short stories, "Please Don't Kill Anything" and "The Prophecy." When Marilyn committed suicide with an overdose of sleeping pills in 1962, Miller refused to attend her funeral because he believed the publicity would turn her tragedy into a "circus." The playwright remained silent.

MILLER IN THE 1960s

During the filming of *The Misfits*, Miller met the woman who would become his third wife, Ingeborg (Inge) Morath. Inge, a Vienna-born photographer, was on the film set to take rehearsal photographs. The daughter of research chemists, Inge was educated in Berlin and worked for a while as the Austrian bureau chief for the magazine *Heute*. Both Marilyn and Arthur liked Inge. Miller was immediately attracted to her independence, her strength of character, and her talent as a photographer. Marilyn Monroe also gravitated to her because of the photographer's kindness and nonaggressive attitude. Marilyn particularly appreciated the fact that Inge portrayed her with great affection and sensitivity. At a time when Miller was obsessed with his failing marriage and his stalled writing career, Inge's confidence and stability must have been very appealing.

Despite Miller's resolve never to marry again, just over a year after his divorce from Monroe, Miller and Morath married in February 1962, six months before Monroe's suicide on August 5. Arthur and Inge would have a daughter, Rebecca, eighteen months later. Miller was extremely happy with Inge, but he was struggling to find the inspiration to write again. The Millers spent most of their time at Roxbury. Here,

Miller worked on his next play, *After the Fall,* his first in nine years. *After the Fall* opened in 1964 at the ANTA Theater–Washington Square. Swamped by preproduction publicity, the play was hyped in the media as not only the reemergence of a great playwright but also a play about Marilyn Monroe. *After the Fall* suffered some of the worst criticism that Miller had ever received. Many critics accused Miller of overusing obvious autobiographical details and shamelessly exploiting his relationship with the popular actress. The main character, Quentin, appears to be Miller himself and the character Maggie, who dies of an overdose of sleeping pills, recalls the recently deceased Monroe. Miller argues that the harsh criticism was inevitable: "I was soon widely hated, but the play had spoken the truth as, after all, it was obliged to do, and if the truth was clothed in pain, perhaps it was important for the audience to confront it uncomfortably and even in the anger of denial." *After the Fall* incorporates the despair of *The Misfits* and contains some of the familiar Miller themes of guilt, self-deception, and the quest for meaning.

Despite the controversy, *After the Fall* played to large audiences and Miller was encouraged by his producers to write another. His new play, *Incident at Vichy,* was written in a very short time and opened in 1964, again to reviews that were generally unfavorable. Based on the story of an analyst friend, Dr. Rudolph Loewenstein, who hid from the Nazis in Vichy France in 1942, the play attacks anti-Semitism. Interestingly, *Incident at Vichy* was not produced in France because of the fear that audiences might resent the implication that the French cooperated with the Nazi attack on the Jews.

MILLER'S FIGHT FOR ARTISTIC FREEDOM

In the mid-1960s Miller's plays were often staged before large audiences in Europe, where the playwright was very popular. As a result, Miller spent a good deal of time in Europe viewing and helping present his work. While in Paris in 1965, Miller was encouraged to become the next president of PEN, an international writers' organization of poets, playwrights, editors, essayists, and novelists. PEN was established after World War I by writers including [George] Bernard Shaw and H.G. Wells to help fight censorship and champion the freedom of writers. Miller was skeptical at first, but after a few days of reflection he agreed to serve as its new leader. Having accepted the responsibility of the PEN presidency, he realized that "willy-nilly, I was pitched into the still indetermi-

nate tangle of detente politics to begin a new and totally un-
expected stage of my learning life."

As the head of PEN for the next four years, Miller dedicated
himself to uplifting the social and political status of writers.
Miller believed that PEN must serve as the conscience of the
world's writing community. Perhaps his dedication to this
task stemmed from his treatment by HUAC, where the playwright learned firsthand that writers are often trapped by political pressures. As did many organizations after World War
II, PEN operated with a cold war mentality that made it un-
compromisingly anti-Soviet. In the sixties, as relations with
Eastern Europe were being reexamined, PEN was finally
making some attempts to enlist and support Soviet writers. As
president, Miller convinced a Soviet delegation, headed by the
Russian writer Alexei Surkov, to join the international organization.

Miller's dedication to PEN and the writers it represented is
exemplified by the fact that Miller delivered a scheduled
speech at the opening of the New York PEN Congress in 1966
despite the fact that his father died that day. Miller found the
strength to deliver the speech because he was convinced that
PEN was the one organization that could apply leverage to
protect the rights of writers internationally. Before he retired
as PEN president in 1969, Miller urged governments around
the world to release writers who were imprisoned for political reasons, particularly in Lithuania, South Africa, Czecho-
slovakia, Latin America, and the Soviet Union.

In 1968 Miller resumed playwriting with *The Price,* a work
about two brothers who cannot overcome their anger with each
other. Reminiscent of his earlier work, *The Price* probes family
relationships, suffocating illusions, and the power of the past to
influence the present. The original staging of the play was beset
by problems that troubled Miller. The director and actors were
caught in a battle of artistic and egotistical differences, the lead
performer dropped out because of illness, and the playwright
himself was eventually enlisted to direct the play during the
week before it opened on Broadway at the Morosco Theater. Despite its problems, the play opened to cordial but generally un-
enthusiastic reviews and ran for 425 performances. At the same
time *The Price* opened, Viking Press, Miller's publisher, awarded
the playwright a gold title page of *Death of a Salesman* to honor
the sale of 1 million copies. This honor emphasizes the fact that
despite the mixed reviews that Miller often received, his audience deeply appreciates the power of his work.

MILLER'S POLITICAL ACTIVISM

Professionally rejuvenated by the success of *The Price*, Miller carried his influence into the arena of politics. Dismayed by the 1963 assassination of President John F. Kennedy, racial inequality, poverty, and the escalating U.S. involvement in Vietnam, Miller accepted the nomination by his fellow Roxbury, Connecticut, Democrats to attend the 1968 Chicago Democratic National Convention as their delegate. Miller went to Chicago to support peace activist Eugene McCarthy and to introduce a resolution on the floor of the convention to cease U.S. bombing in Vietnam. When his resolution was rejected, Miller wrote that he "felt totally defeated by the absence of any spoken word commemorating the long fight to end the war, and by the abdication of the men who had led the struggle within the Democratic Party and were now allowing it to vanish ... unmourned and unsung." The convention itself turned chaotic and the antiwar protests outside the convention hall turned violent as the Chicago police clashed with protesters. This experience seemed to cap Miller's fear that values in America were breaking down, violence was becoming epidemic, and government was acting with increased paranoia and force.

Reflecting on his political activism in *Timebends: A Life*, the playwright states that "the sixties was a time of stalemate for me. . . . I could find no refreshing current of history such as I had imagined touching in the thirties and forties, only a moral stagnation that mocked creation itself." Nevertheless, Miller reaffirmed his need to write social drama because, despite the chaos of the age, the common people "still wanted better lives for their kids, wished marriages could last, and clung to a certain biological decency."

MILLER IN THE 1970S

In the 1970s Miller wrote three plays: *The Creation of the World and Other Business* (1972), *The American Clock* (1976), and *The Archbishop's Ceiling* (1977). The productions of all three works were harshly criticized. *The Creation of the World and Other Business* closed after only twenty performances; *The Archbishop's Ceiling* had a short life at Washington's Kennedy Center. However, like a delayed reaction, both *The American Clock* and *The Archbishop's Ceiling* found a receptive audience in London during the mid-1980s.

Throughout the 1970s Miller continued to fight tirelessly for the rights of individuals and the freedom of writers. For example, he helped free Brazilian writer Augusto Boal, imprisoned for his political beliefs. In 1972 Miller publicly criticized the three-year sentence given to publisher Ralph Ginzburg for an obscenity conviction that was appealed all the way to the U.S. Supreme Court. Because of a letter to Miller from famous Czech poet and playwright Pavel Kohout, Miller organized fifty-three other writers and literary figures to sign a written statement sent to the Czech leaders protesting their arrest of dissident thinkers. Miller was a major voice in the process to free dissident Russian writer Aleksandr Solzhenitsyn, whose moral strength Miller had compared to that of John Proctor in *The Crucible.* For his effort, the Soviet government banned all of Miller's works. The irony was not lost on Miller, who pointed out that his plays had been under attack by his own government for his suspected Communist sympathies and that now the Soviet government had banned his work for pushing American-style individual rights.

Perhaps the best example of Miller's involvement in the struggle of the individual against governmental authority is found in the case of Peter Reilly, who was convicted of brutally slashing his mother's throat in Canaan, Connecticut, in 1973. The case came to Miller's attention two years later when he read the transcript of Reilly's interrogation. Miller, like the friends and neighbors of the Reilly family, felt that the police had methodically and cynically broken the will of the exhausted and frightened young Peter and forced him to sign a confession. Miller enlisted the help of a lawyer friend and a private investigator to reopen the case, bring about a new trial, and ultimately free Peter Reilly. The Reilly case was a perfect cause for the playwright who had for so long concerned himself with individual rights, the abuse of authority, the perplexing nature of truth, and the themes of justice and morality. The Reilly case also reflects Miller's fascination with the law. To the playwright, who includes a lawyer in almost all of his plays, the law is the last defense against society's inability to see or accept the truth. Reflecting on the case in his autobiography, Miller writes, "If the long months of the Reilly case left a darkened picture of man, it was no less perplexing for being accompanied by the most unlikely examples of courage and goodness, of people rising to the occasion when there was little reason to expect they would."

MILLER'S REVIVAL IN THE 1980s

During the eighties Arthur Miller's works experienced a worldwide revival. Shortly after *A View from the Bridge* opened on Broadway in 1983, Miller and his wife traveled to Beijing, China, to see a production of *Death of a Salesman*. In Beijing the audience responded positively to the elementary human concerns dramatically portrayed in *Death of a Salesman*. Miller writes in his autobiography that "the Chinese reaction to my Beijing production of *Salesman* would confirm what had become more and more obvious over the decades in the play's hundreds of productions throughout the world: Willy was representative everywhere, in every kind of system, of ourselves in this time."

In 1984 the revival continued on Broadway with the opening of *Death of a Salesman* starring Dustin Hoffman as Willy Loman. Dustin Hoffman also played the lead in the 1985 CBS televised production of the play, which was broadcast to an audience of more than 25 million viewers. In addition, *The Price* was successfully revived on Broadway and in 1989 *The Crucible*, directed by Arvin Brown, was staged in New Haven. America was beginning to understand Arthur Miller's contribution to American theater, art, and consciousness. This recognition of his long and prolific career climaxed when Miller won the Kennedy Center Honors award for distinguished lifetime achievement in 1984. At the award banquet a powerful irony struck the playwright; the ceremony was held in the same room in which Miller faced the House Un-American Activities Committee almost thirty years earlier.

CONCLUSION

Miller's most recent plays have not enjoyed successful theatrical runs. In 1991 his play *The Ride Down Mt. Morgan* premiered in London, but ran for only three months. His latest play, *The Last Yankee*, a comedy-drama, also suffered a short life span after it opened in 1993 at the Manhattan Theatre Club in New York. Now in his eighties, Miller is still working.

In his autobiography, it is apparent that the experiences of Miller's life have merged with his artistic goals to create a very personal body of work. The impact of his family, the depression, his discovery of drama at the University of Michigan, his unfortunate standoff with HUAC, his marriages, his political activism as president of PEN, his protest of the war in Vietnam, and his ongoing relationship with the theater, its critics, and its audiences have all coalesced to shape the form and power of his plays.

The characters in Miller's dramas act out human concerns that engage the playwright personally. He calls on his characters to take responsibility for their actions, and Miller himself never shies away from his responsibility to act on his own convictions. Miller rejects self-pity in his characters, and he consistently rebounds from harsh criticism. Miller wants his characters to find the strength to overcome moral paralysis and act on the world, and Miller sticks to his moral beliefs against popular opinion. In a sense Miller is similar to Ben in *Death of a Salesman*—he went into the "jungle" and came out a success; he did not succumb to the nullifying illusions that defeated Willy Loman. He carried on a dialogue with himself, his family, and his audience that continues to this day. Miller lives with his wife Inge at the same home in Roxbury, Connecticut, that he purchased after the success of *All My Sons*. He is a grandfather to his son's three children; his two daughters, Rebecca and Jane, are both involved in the arts; and his wife's love of photography continues.

Throughout his career, Miller's works reveal the idea that beneath the chaos of reality there are hidden forces that connect all human beings to one another and to the world. It is with this major theme that Miller chooses to end his autobiography. Pondering the coyotes that he can see outside his Roxbury studio window, Miller writes, "I am a mystery to them until they tire of it and move on, but the truth, the first truth, probably, is that we are all connected, watching one another." As thousands of audiences watch the interior workings of Arthur Miller unfold on stage, the playwright moves them to wonder about that truth.

CHAPTER 1

Historical Background of *The Crucible*

READINGS ON
THE CRUCIBLE

The Historical Basis of
The Crucible

June Schlueter and James K. Flanagan

According to scholars June Schlueter and James K. Flanagan, *The Crucible* is accurately based on the historical events of the Salem witchcraft trials, but, as a dramatist, Miller shapes the material to suit his dramatic purpose. For example, the playwright invents the relationship between Abigail Williams and John Proctor. Miller uses history to portray society at its tyrannical worst, exposing fraud, faulty logic, vindictiveness, zealotry, and evil.

Schlueter and Flanagan also discuss the parallels between the play and the national mania that emerged from the Communist hunt of Senator Joseph McCarthy in the 1950s. They argue that although Miller saw the two events as analogous, he viewed the Salem witch trials as something more than the political madness of McCarthyism. Miller characterized the Salem event as an expression of a deep communal and personal guilt by which participants of a repressive society found release in publicly expressing their sins.

June Schlueter is an associate professor of English at Lafayette College in Easton, Pennsylvania. She is the editor of *Feminist Re-Readings of Modern American Drama* and *Metafictional Characters in Modern Drama* and has contributed articles and reviews to numerous journals including *Comparative Drama* and *Modern Drama.* James K. Flanagan contributed portions of his doctoral dissertation for Schlueter's work.

The Crucible is patterned in a detailed and accurate manner upon the historical records of the Salem witchcraft trials of 1692. As a consequence of the fanaticism that characterized those trials, nineteen women and men and two dogs were hanged, one man was pressed to death for refusing to plead, and 150 were imprisoned; they were awaiting trial when a Boston court finally declared the evidence insufficient to warrant the death sentence. Communal participation in the witch-hunts was in response to the testimony of a group of girls and young women, aged nine to twenty, who fainted and cried out in hysteria as they named their prey. In "A Note on the Historical Accuracy of This Play," Miller observes that the fates of the characters in *The Crucible* coincide with those of their historical counterparts. In order to shape the historical material to suit his dramatic purpose, however, he made a number of minor alterations, at times representing several characters as one or two, as with the court officials, Hathorne and Danforth; reducing the number of girls involved in the witch naming; and, to make credible the invented relationship between Abigail Williams and John Proctor, turning a preadolescent girl into a seventeen-year-old.

HISTORICAL CHARACTERS IN *THE CRUCIBLE*

Miller speaks as well of the historical characters and circumstances in Salem through a lengthy narrative beginning act 1 and through interruptive narrations throughout that act. The historical Parris, a fatherless widower with little understanding of or love for children, "cut a villainous path," apparently the consequence of a persecution complex. Thomas Putnam, son of the richest man in Salem, sought restitution for the village's rejection of his candidate for minister and contested his father's will when it favored his younger brother; Putnam's name appeared on a number of historical documents, characterizing him as an embittered, vindictive man. Francis Nurse was a frequent arbitrator in Salem, a man apparently capable of impartial judgment; he was, however, involved in a land dispute with his neighbors, including Putnam, and in the campaign for the ministerial candidate in opposition to Putnam's. It was Putnam who initiated the document accusing the highly respected Rebecca Nurse, Francis's wife, of witchcraft, and Putnam's young daughter who pointed hysterically and accusingly at the old woman at the hearing. Giles Corey, a man in his eighties at the time of the hearings, was the village misfit; careless of public opinion and casual about religion, he was the first to be suspected when a cow was missing or a fire blazed. And John Proctor, a farmer, was "the kind of man—powerful of body, even-tempered, and not easily led—who cannot refuse support to partisans without drawing their deepest resentment. In Proctor's presence a fool felt his foolishness instantly—and a Proctor is always marked for calumny therefore." But none of the personal animosities and motives of those involved in the purge at Salem seemed to be the concern of the court, which pursued its cause with a dedication and a zeal that repeatedly endorsed Salem's heritage of "self-denial," "purposefulness," "suspicion of all vain pursuits," and "hard-handed justice."

Miller knew his dramatization of the Salem trials portrayed society at its tyrannical worst, polarizing good and evil so that, for his audience, those who opted to save their lives were clearly moral cowards and those who hanged were heroes. Abigail, absent the idealism she expressed in the forest, was unquestionably a fraud, whose missionary zeal, though in tune with the genuine zeal of the court, was unconscionable. And the court's officials as well, guardians of a misguided society's propensity for purity, carried out their grim task with an energy and a dedication that a contemporary audience could only associate with animated evil. Danforth and Hathorne, who presided over the court, and the early Hale possessed and perpetuated a simplistic mentality that functioned in polarities and in the assurance of right.

Though such insistence upon absolute evil diminishes the complexity of moral decision, Miller, in reflecting on *The Crucible*, was sorry he did not emphasize the polarities even more:

> I think now, almost four years after the writing of it, that I was wrong in mitigating the evil of this man [Danforth] and the judges he represents. Instead, I would perfect his evil to its utmost and make an open issue, a thematic consideration of it in the play. I believe now, as I did not conceive then, that there are people dedicated to evil in the world; that without their perverse example we should not know the good.

McCarthyism and the Salem Witch-Hunt Analogy

The occasion for Miller's writing of *The Crucible* was clearly the specter of McCarthyism that possessed America at the time. In 1950, Senator Joseph McCarthy of Wisconsin publicly charged that 205 communists had infiltrated the state department. Though he could not name a single card-carrying communist, McCarthy transformed his strident voice into a national mania. Before he was censured in late

1954 by his own Senate colleagues, he had assassinated the
characters and ruined the professional lives of a host of
Americans, whom he accused of having communist sympa-
thies. The zealous guardian of the public good led a vulnerable country through one of the darkest chapters in its history.

The analogy between the McCarthy communist hunt and
the Salem witch-hunt was clearly fundamental to Miller's
dramatic strategy. But despite the effectiveness of the strategy—not to mention the artistic courage such a political action endorsed—Eric Bentley saw the analogy as erroneous;
writing in 1953, he noted that, unlike witchcraft, "communism is not . . . merely a chimera." Indeed, no one knew this
better than Miller, who not only made the same acknowl-
edgment in his narrative in the play but who was himself
called before the House Committee on Un-American Activities three years after the opening of *The Crucible.* Facing an
investigative process similar to that in Salem, Miller, unlike
many of his contemporaries, survived professionally, escap-
ing involvement in the ritualistic terror of exposing names of
so-called communist subversives.

In the introduction to *Collected Plays,* Miller observed that
the climate in this country immediately preceding Mc-
Carthyism was one of a "new religiosity," an "official piety"
that created new sins monthly and "above all horrors . . . accepted the notion that conscience was no longer a private
matter but one of state administration." But his attraction to
the Salem witchcraft trials preceded his writing of *The Crucible* by some years. More than the specific, contemporary
political madness, Miller saw in the Salem witch-hunts a
model of the subtle but devastating usurpation of political
purity by the religious mentality. The Salem affair was em-
blematic of a presiding communal and personal guilt that
the hysteria did not create but unleashed. A repressive society, Salem endorsed an austere life of self-denial that was
enforced by communally created laws dedicated to preserv-
ing order and public authority.

But individual, personal guilt figured strongly in Miller's
drama as well. If the historical Salem court ignored personal
animosity, Miller's play repeatedly suggests impure motives,
creating quarrels between Proctor and Parris over whether
the minister's firewood should be included in his salary and
between Proctor and Putnam over a piece of land, creating
jealousy on the part of Abigail over Elizabeth and suspicion

on the part of Elizabeth over her husband and Abigail. Abigail's animosity toward Elizabeth is a clear example of a vindictiveness that Abigail has been unable, for seven months, to express any more effectively than in her response to Parris's early query. There she imputed hatred and bitterness to Abigail, defending her own good name and calling Goody Proctor a "gossiping liar." Through Tituba's confession, Miller more subtly suggests the extent to which repressed desire found a forum in the Salem witch-hunts. When forced to admit her relationship with the devil, Tituba immediately charges the devil with discrediting Parris, coaxing her into killing him, just as, the confession implies, Tituba might have liked to have done.

THE ROLE OF GUILT IN THE PLAY

As Miller points out, the witch-hunt was "a long overdue opportunity for everyone so inclined to express publicly his guilt and sins, under the cover of accusations against the victims." For those who confessed to trafficking with the devil, the witchcraft hearings provided both an opportunity to articulate guilt in a specific form and a forum for expression. In a society that nurtures through its repressiveness an abiding sense of personal guilt, there is freedom in falling to one's knees and agreeing to the most heinous of sins, face-to-face communion with evil. It is not difficult to imagine members of the Salem community secretly hoping their names would be the next to be called, for in such a climate people not only want others to be guilty, they want their own guilt recognized as well, even as they fear the consequence.

Like [Norwegian dramatist Henrik] Ibsen, Miller has always been interested in the question of guilt; in *All My Sons*, he examined the toxic consequences of hidden culpability on the part of the head of a family. But Joe Keller is guilty of a specific crime of commission; for other Miller characters, including many in *The Crucible*, guilt is a less specific quality of mind. When urged into communal expression by a public forum, such guilt acquires enormous power. [Literary critic] Dennis Welland rightly observes that "in the life of a society evil is occasioned less by deliberate villainy than by the abnegation of personal responsibility," by the failure of the individual to assert and define his sense of self-worth. Such guilt, which Miller will repeatedly acknowledge and examine in his subsequent work, greatly inhibits that defense.

The Use of Salem's Historical Record in *The Crucible*

Arthur Miller

In the following article Arthur Miller writes that *The Crucible* is about how public terror robs an individual of his conscience and how guilt kills an individual's personality.

While studying Salem's historical record, the playwright wondered why Abigail, who had worked for the Proctors, wanted to convict Elizabeth of being a witch but not John. Miller speculated that John had taken Abigail as a mistress. The playwright uses John's guilt for this indiscretion as the human focal point of the play and as the motivating force that ultimately drives Proctor's moral outcry against Salem's hysteria.

Miller also argues that Salem's authorities demonstrated a very real dedication to evil. He argues that this absolute evil was neither misplaced good nor misdirected intentions; rather, it was calculated and sadistic. In his play Miller wants to show the audience that it is possible for otherwise normal individuals to act evilly.

Arthur Miller is an American playwright, novelist, and short story writer. His Pulitzer Prize–winning drama *Death of a Salesman* and his widely produced play *The Crucible* make Miller one of America's most influential modern dramatists.

I wished for a way to write a play that would be sharp, that would lift out of the morass of subjectivism the squirming, single, defined process which would show that the sin of public terror is that it divests man of conscience, of himself. It was a theme not unrelated to those that had invested the previous plays. In *The Crucible*, however, there was an attempt to move beyond the discovery and unveiling of the hero's guilt, a guilt that kills the personality. I had grown increasingly conscious of this theme in my past work, and aware too that it was no longer enough for me to build a play, as it were, upon the revelation of guilt, and to rely solely upon a fate which exacts payment from the culpable man. Now guilt appeared to me no longer the bedrock beneath which the probe could not penetrate. I saw it now as a betrayer, as possibly the most real of our illusions, but nevertheless a quality of mind capable of being overthrown.

THE CENTRAL RELATIONSHIP OF JOHN, ABIGAIL, AND ELIZABETH

I had known of the Salem witch hunt for many years before "McCarthyism" had arrived, and it had always remained an inexplicable darkness to me. When I looked into it now, however, it was with the contemporary situation at my back, particularly the mystery of the handing over of conscience which seemed to me the central and informing fact of the time. One finds, I suppose, what one seeks. I doubt I should ever have tempted agony by actually writing a play on the subject had I not come upon a single fact. It was that Abigail Williams, the prime mover of the Salem hysteria, so far as the hysterical children were concerned, had a short time earlier been the house servant of the Proctors and now was crying out Elizabeth Proctor as a witch; but more—it was clear from the record that with entirely uncharacteristic fastidiousness she was refusing to include John Proctor, Elizabeth's husband, in her accusations despite the urgings of the prosecutors. Why? I searched the records of the trials in the courthouse at Salem but in no other instance could I find such a careful avoidance of the implicating stutter, the murderous, ambivalent answer to the sharp questions of the prosecutors. Only here, in Proctor's case, was there so clear an attempt to differentiate between a wife's culpability and a husband's.

The testimony of Proctor himself is one of the least elaborate in the records, and Elizabeth is not one of the major cases either. There could have been numerous reasons for his having been ultimately apprehended and hanged which are nowhere to be found. After the play opened, several of his descendants wrote to me; and one of them believes that

Proctor fell under suspicion because, according to family tradition, he had for years been an amateur inventor whose machines appeared to some people as devilish in their ingenuity, and—again according to tradition—he had to conceal them and work on them privately long before the witch hunt had started, for fear of censure if not worse. The explanation does not account for everything, but it does fall in with his evidently liberated cast of mind as revealed in the record; he was one of the few who not only refused to admit consorting with evil spirits, but who persisted in calling the entire business a ruse and a fake. Most, if not all, of the other victims were of their time in conceding the existence of the immemorial plot by the Devil to take over the visible world, their only reservation being that they happened not to have taken part in it themselves.

It was the fact that Abigail, their former servant, was their accuser, and her apparent desire to convict Elizabeth and save John, that made the play conceivable for me.

As in any such mass phenomenon, the number of characters of vital, if not decisive, importance is so great as to make the dramatic problem excessively difficult. For a time it seemed best to approach the town impressionistically, and, by a mosaic of seemingly disconnected scenes, gradually to form a context of cause and effect. This I believe I might well have done had it not been that the central impulse for writing at all was not the social but the interior psychological question, which was the question of that guilt residing in Salem which the hysteria merely unleashed, but did not create. Consequently, the structure reflects that understanding, and it centers in John, Elizabeth, and Abigail.

THE FORCE OF EVIL IN THE HISTORICAL RECORD AND THE PLAY

In reading the record, which was taken down verbatim at the trial, I found one recurring note which had a growing effect upon my concept, not only of the phenomenon itself, but of our modern way of thinking about people, and especially of the treatment of evil in contemporary drama. Some critics have taken exception, for instance, to the unrelieved badness of the prosecution in my play. I understand how this is possible, and I plead no mitigation, but I was up against historical facts which were immutable. I do not think that either the record itself or the numerous commentaries upon it reveal any mitigation of the unrelieved, straightforward, and absolute dedication to evil displayed by the judges of these trials and the prosecutors. After days of study it became quite incredible how perfect they were in this respect. I recall, almost as in a dream, how Rebecca Nurse, a pious and universally respected woman of great age, was literally taken by force from her sickbed and ferociously cross-examined. No human weakness could be displayed without the prosecution's stabbing into it with greater fury. The most patent contradictions, almost laughable even in that day, were overridden with warnings not to repeat their mention. There was a sadism here that was breathtaking.

So much so, that I sought but could not at the time take hold of a concept of man which might really begin to account for such evil. For instance, it seems beyond doubt that members of the Putnam family consciously, coldly, and with malice aforethought conferred in private with some of the girls, and told them whom it was desirable to cry out upon next. There is and will always be in my mind the spectacle of the great minister, and ideological authority behind the prosecution, Cotton Mather, galloping up to the scaffold to beat back a crowd of villagers so moved by the towering dignity of the victims as to want to free them.

It was not difficult to foresee the objections to such absolute evil in men; we are committed, after all, to the belief that it does not and cannot exist. Had I this play to write now, however, I might proceed on an altered concept. I should say that my own—and the critics'—unbelief in this depth of evil is concomitant with our unbelief in good, too. I should now examine this fact of evil as such. Instead, I sought to make Danforth, for instance, perceptible as a human being by showing him somewhat put off by Mary Warren's turnabout at the height of the trials, which caused no little confusion. In my play, Danforth seems about to conceive of the truth, and surely there is a disposition in him at least to listen to arguments that go counter to the line of the prosecution. There is no such swerving in the record, and I think now, almost four years after the writing of it, that I was wrong in mitigating the evil of this man and the judges he represents. Instead, I would perfect his evil to its utmost and make an open issue, a thematic consideration of it in the play. I believe now, as I did not conceive then, that there are people dedicated to evil in the world; that without their perverse example we should not know the good. Evil is not a mistake but a fact in itself. I have never proceeded psychoanalytically in my thought, but neither have I been separated from that humane if not humanistic conception of man as being essentially innocent while the evil in him represents but a perversion of his frustrated love. I posit no metaphysical force of evil which totally possesses certain individuals, nor do I even deny that given infinite wisdom and patience and knowledge any human being can be saved from himself. I believe merely that, from whatever cause, a dedication to evil, not mistaking it for good, but knowing it as evil and loving it as evil, is possible in human beings who appear agreeable and normal. I think now that one of the hidden weaknesses of our whole approach to dramatic psychology is our inability to face this fact—to conceive, in effect, of Iago.[1]

MORAL AWARENESS OF THE CHARACTERS

The Crucible is a "tough" play. My criticism of it now would be that it is not tough enough. I say this not merely out of deference to the record of these trials, but out of a consideration for drama. We are so intent upon getting sympathy for our characters that the consequences of evil are being muddied by sentimentality under the guise of a temperate weighing of causes. The tranquility of the bad man lies at the heart of not only moral philosophy but dramaturgy as well. But my central intention in this play was to one side of this idea, which was realized only as the play was in production. All I sought here was to take a step not only beyond the realization of guilt, but beyond the helpless victimization of the hero.

The society of Salem was "morally" vocal. People then avowed principles, sought to live by them and die by them. Issues of faith, conduct, society, pervaded their private lives in a conscious way. They needed but to disapprove to act. I was drawn to this subject because the historical moment seemed to give me the poetic right to create people of higher self-awareness than the contemporary scene affords. I had explored the subjective world in *Salesman* and I wanted now to move closer to a conscious hero.

The decidedly mixed reception to the play was not easily traceable, but I believe there are causes for it which are of

1. the villain in Shakespeare's *Othello*

moment to more than this play alone. I believe that the very moral awareness of the play and its characters—which are historically correct—was repulsive to the audience. For a variety of reasons I think that the Anglo-Saxon audience cannot believe the reality of characters who live by principles and know very much about their own characters and situations, and who say what they know. Our drama, for this among other reasons, is condemned, so to speak, to the emotions of subjectivism, which, as they approach knowledge and self-awareness, become less and less actual and real to us. In retrospect I think that my course in *The Crucible* should have been toward greater self-awareness and not, as my critics have implied, toward an enlarged and more pervasive subjectivism. The realistic form and style of the play would then have had to give way. What new form might have evolved I cannot now say, but certainly the passion of knowing is as powerful as the passion of feeling alone, and the writing of the play broached the question of that new form for me.

The work of Bertolt Brecht[2] inevitably rises up in any such quest. It seems to me that, while I cannot agree with his concept of the human situation, his solution of the problem of consciousness is admirably honest and theatrically powerful. One cannot watch his productions without knowing that he is at work not on the periphery of the contemporary dramatic problem, but directly upon its center—which is again the problem of consciousness.

THE CRUCIBLE AS REALIST DRAMA

The Crucible, then, opened up a new prospect, and, like every work when completed, it left behind it unfinished business. It made a new freedom possible, and it also threw a certain light upon the difference between the modern play-writing problem of meaning and that of the age preceding the secularization of society. It is impossible to study the trial record without feeling the immanence of a veritable pantheon of life values in whose name both prosecution and defense could speak. The testimony is thick with reference to Biblical examples, and even as religious belief did nothing to temper cruelty—and in fact might be shown to have made the cruel crueler—it often served to raise this swirling and ludicrous mysticism to a level of high moral debate; and it

2. German dramatist

did this despite the fact that most of the participants were unlettered, simple folk. They lived and would die more in the shadow of the other world than in the light of this one (and it is no mean irony that the theocratic prosecution should seek out the most religious people for its victims).

The longer I dwelt on the whole spectacle, the more clear became the failure of the present age to find a universal moral sanction, and the power of realism's hold on our theater was an aspect of this vacuum. For it began to appear that our inability to break more than the surfaces of realism reflected our inability—playwrights and audiences—to agree upon the pantheon of forces and values which must lie behind the realistic surfaces of life. In this light, realism, as a style, could seem to be a defense against the assertion of meaning. How strange a conclusion this is when one realizes that the same style seventy years ago was the prime instrument of those who sought to illuminate meaning in the theater, who divested their plays of fancy talk and improbable locales and bizarre characters in order to bring "life" onto the stage. And I wondered then what was true. Was it that we had come to fear the hard glare of life on the stage and under the guise of an aesthetic surfeited with realism were merely expressing our flight from reality? Or was our condemned realism only the counterfeit of the original, whose most powerful single impetus was to deal with man as a social animal? Any form can be drained of its informing purpose, can be used to convey, like the Tudor façades of college dormitories, the now vanished dignity and necessity of a former age in order to lend specious justification for a present hollowness. Was it realism that stood in the way of meaning or was it the counterfeit of realism?

Increasingly over the past five years and more the poetic plays, so-called, some of them much admired by all sorts of critics, were surprisingly full of what in the university years ago was called "fine" writing. If one heard less of the creak of plot machinery there was more of the squeak of self-pity, the humming of the poetic poseur, the new romance of the arbitrary and the uncompleted. For one, I had seen enough of the "borrowings" of the set, the plot, the time-shifting methods, and the lighting of *Death of a Salesman* to have an intimate understanding of how a vessel could be emptied and still purveyed to the public as new wine. Was realism called futile now because it needed to illuminate an exact meaning behind it, a conviction that was no more with us? Confusion, the inability to describe one's sense of a thing, often issues in a genuine poetry of feeling, and feeling was now raised up as the highest good and the ultimate attainment in drama. I had known that kind of victory myself with *Salesman;* but was there not another realm even higher, where feeling took awareness more openly by the hand and both equally ruled and were illuminated? I had found a kind of self-awareness in the bloody book of Salem and had thought that since the natural, realistic surface of that society was one already immersed in the questions of meaning and the relations of men to God, to write a realistic play of that world was already to write in a style beyond contemporary realism. That more than one critic had found the play "cold" when I had never written more passionately was by this time an acceptable and inevitable detail of my fate, for, while it will never confess to it, our theater is trained—actors, directors, audience, and critics—to take to its heart anything that does not prick the mind and to suspect everything that does not supinely reassure.

Miller's Manipulation of Fact Results in Powerful Drama

Robert A. Martin

Robert A. Martin approaches *The Crucible* as a cultural and historical study rather than a political allegory of the 1950s McCarthy hearings. Martin suggests that the characters in the play are compressed representations of the underlying forces of hatred, fear, and hysteria. For example, Miller compresses several girls from the Salem historical record into the character of Abigail. Her focused hatred of Proctor's wife, Elizabeth, reflects a wider hatred and tension in the Salem community. Similarly, Martin concludes that the forces of social malfunction are represented in Reverend John Hale. With Hale the witchcraft controversy moves from an unofficial local issue to an official theological inquiry. Although he was tormented with doubts about the trials, five years later the historical Hale concluded that though the trials were unfortunate the judges were trying to do what was right.

Martin explains that the first accused witches were old and eccentric women like Sarah Good, but soon the trials took a different turn when people like Rebecca Nurse and John Proctor were accused. Martin argues that the historical Proctor was more a victim of the laws than Miller's Proctor. His property and goods were confiscated even before his trial and conviction, indicating that neither John nor Elizabeth were expected to return from prison. Martin claims that all the judges involved in the Salem trials were symbolized in Danforth and Hathorne. Historically, the hangings stopped due to a legal question concerning the reliability of spectral evidence based on the testimony of the afflicted.

Robert A. Martin is professor of English at the University

Reprinted from "Arthur Miller's *The Crucible*: Background and Sources," by Robert A. Martin, *Modern Drama*, vol. 20, no. 3 (November 1977), pp. 279–90, by permission of *Modern Drama*.

of Michigan, Ann Arbor. He is the editor of *The Theater Essays of Arthur Miller* and a contributor of numerous theater articles in such periodical as *Modern Drama, Educational Theatre Journal, Michigan Quarterly Review* and *Studies in American Fiction.*

When *The Crucible* opened on January 22, 1953, the term "witch-hunt" was nearly synonymous in the public mind with the Congressional investigations then being conducted into allegedly subversive activities. Arthur Miller's plays have always been closely identified with contemporary issues, and to many observers the parallel between the witchcraft trials at Salem, Massachusetts in 1692 and the current Congressional hearings was the central issue of the play.

Miller has said that he could not have written *The Crucible* at any other time, a statement which reflects both his reaction to the McCarthy era and the creative process by which he finds his way to the thematic center of a play. If it is true, however, that a play cannot be successful in its own time unless it speaks to its own time, it is also true that a play cannot endure unless it speaks to new audiences in new times. The latter truism may apply particularly to *The Crucible*, which is presently being approached more and more frequently as a cultural and historical study rather than as a political allegory. . . .

The events that eventually found their way into *The Crucible* are largely contained in the massive two-volume record of the trials located in the Essex County Archives at Salem, Massachusetts, where Miller went to do his research. Although he has been careful to point out in a prefatory note that *The Crucible* is not history in the academic sense, a study of the play and its sources indicates that Miller did his research carefully and well. He found in the records of the trials at Salem that between June 10 and September 22, 1692, nineteen men and women and two dogs were hanged for witchcraft, and one man was pressed to death for standing mute. Before the affair ended, fifty-five people had confessed to being witches, and another hundred and fifty were in jail awaiting trial. . . .

CHARACTERIZATION IN *THE CRUCIBLE*

With the exception of Abigail and Proctor's adultery, the events and characters of *The Crucible* are not so much "invented" data in a fictional sense as highly compressed representations

of the underlying forces of hatred, hysteria, and fear that para-
lyzed Salem during the spring and summer of 1692. And even
in this context Abigail Williams's characterization in the play
may be more restrained in the light of the records than Miller's
dramatization suggests. For example, one of the major witnesses against John Proctor was twelve-year-old Ann Putnam,
who testified on June 30 that "on the day of his examination I
saw the apparition of John Proctor senior go and afflict and
most grievously torture the bodies of Mistress Pope, Mary Walcott, Mercy Lewis, Abigail Williams. . . ." In projecting several
of the girls into Abigail, Miller has used the surface of the trial
records to suggest that her hatred for Proctor's wife is a dramatic equivalent for the much wider spread hatred and tension that existed within the Salem community. Abigail, although morally corrupt, ironically insists upon her "good"
name, and reveals at an early point in the play that she hates
Elizabeth Proctor for ruining her reputation:

> PARRIS. [*to the point*] Abigail, is there any other cause than you
> have told me, for your being discharged from Goody Proctor's
> service? I have heard it said, and I tell you as I heard it, that
> she comes so rarely to the church this year for she will not sit
> so close to something soiled. What signified that remark?
>
> ABIGAIL. She hates me uncle, she must, for I would not be her
> slave. It's a bitter woman, a lying, cold, sniveling woman, and
> I will not work for such a woman!

On a larger scale, Miller brings together the forces of personal and social malfunction through the arrival of the Reverend John Hale, who appears, appropriately, in the midst of a
bitter quarrel among Proctor, Parris, and Thomas Putnam over
deeds and land boundaries. Hale, in life as in the play, had encountered witchcraft previously and was called to Salem to determine if the Devil was in fact responsible for the illness of the
afflicted children. In the play, he conceives of himself, Miller
says, "much as a young doctor on his first call":

> [*He appears loaded down with half a dozen heavy books.*]
>
> HALE. Pray you, someone take these!
>
> PARRIS. [*delighted*] Mr. Hale! Oh! it's good to see you again!
> [*Taking some books*] My, they're heavy!
>
> HALE. [*setting down his books*] They must be; they are
> weighted with authority.

Hale's entrance at this particular point in the play is significant
in that he interrupts an argument based on private and secu-

lar interests to bring "authority" to the question of witchcraft. His confidence in himself and his subsequent examination of the girls and Tituba (Parris's slave who inadvertently started the entire affair) represent and foreshadow the arrival of outside religious authority in the community. As an outsider who has come to weigh the evidence, Hale also helps to elevate the issue from a local to a regional level, and from an unofficial to an official theological inquiry. His heavy books of authority also symbolically anticipate the heavy authority of the judges who, as he will realize too late, are as susceptible to misinterpreting testimony based on spectral evidence as he is:

> HALE. [*with a tasty love of intellectual pursuit*] Here is all the invisible world, caught, defined, and calculated. In these books the Devil stands stripped of all his brute disguises. Here are all your familiar spirits—your incubi and succubi; your witches that go by land, by air, and by sea; your wizards of the night and of the day. Have no fear now—we shall find him out if he has come among us, and I mean to crush him utterly if he has shown his face!

THE HISTORICAL REVEREND HALE

The Reverend Hale is an extremely interesting figure historically, and following the trials he set down an account of his repentance entitled "A Modest Inquiry into the Nature of Witchcraft" (Boston, 1702). Although he was at first as overly zealous in his pursuit of witches as everyone else, very much as Miller has portrayed him in *The Crucible*, Hale began to be tormented by doubts early in the proceedings. His uncertainty concerning the reliability of the witnesses and their testimony was considerably heightened when his own wife was also accused of being a witch. Hale appears to have been as tortured spiritually and as dedicated to the "middle way" in his later life as Miller has portrayed him in *The Crucible*. Five years after Salem, he wrote in his "Inquiry":

> The middle way is commonly the way of truth. And if any can shew me a better middle way than I have here laid down, I shall be ready to embrace it: But the conviction must not be by vinegar or drollery, but by strength of argument. . . . I have had a deep sence of the sad consequence of mistakes in matters Capital; and their impossibility of recovering when compleated. And what grief of heart it brings to a tender conscience, to have been unwittingly encouraging of the Sufferings of the innocent.

Hale further commented that although he presently believed the executions to be the unfortunate result of human error, the integrity of the court officials was unquestionable: "I observed in the prosecution of these affairs, that there was in the Justices, Judges and others concerned, a conscientious endeavour to do the thing that was right. And to that end they consulted the Presidents [Precedents] of former times and precepts laid down by Learned Writers about Witchcraft."

In *The Crucible*, Hale's examination of Tituba is very nearly an edited transcription of her testimony at the trial of Sarah Good, who is the first person Abigail accuses of consorting with the Devil. At the time of the trials, Sarah Good had long been an outcast member of the Salem community, "unpopular because of her slothfulness, her sullen temper, and her poverty; she had recently taken to begging, an occupation the Puritans detested." When she was about to be hanged, her minister, the Reverend Nicholas Noyes, made a last appeal to her for a confession and said he knew she was a witch. Her prophetic reply was probably seen later as proof of her guilt when she said to Noyes: "you are a lyer; I am no more a Witch than you are a Wizard, and if you take away my Life, God will give you Blood to drink." A few years after she was hanged, Reverend Noyes died as a result of a sudden and severe hemorrhage.

Largely through the Reverend Hale, Miller reflects the change that took place in Salem from an initial belief in the justice of the court to a suspicion that testimony based on spectral evidence was insufficient for execution. This transformation begins to reveal itself in Act Two, as Hale tells Francis Nurse that the court will clear his wife of the charges against her: "Believe me, Mr. Nurse, if Rebecca Nurse be tainted, then nothing's left to stop the whole green world from burning. Let you rest upon the justice of the court; the court will send her home, I know it." By Act Three, however, Hale's confidence in the justice of the court has been badly shaken by the arrest and conviction of people like Rebecca Nurse who were highly respected members of the church and community. Hale, like his historical model, has discovered that "the whole green world" is burning indeed, and fears that he has helped to set the fire.

Partially as a result of Hale's preliminary investigation into the reality of Salem witchcraft, the Court of Oyer and Terminer was appointed to hear testimony and conduct the examinations. The members of the court immediately encountered a serious obstacle: namely, that although the Bible does not define witchcraft, it states unequivocally that "Thou shalt not suffer a witch to live" (Exodus 22:18). As Proctor attempts to save his wife from hanging, Hale attempts to save his conscience by demanding visible proof of the guilt of those who have been convicted on the basis of spectral testimony:

> HALE. Excellency, I have signed seventy-two death warrants; I am a minister of the Lord, and I dare not take a life without there be a proof so immaculate no slightest qualm of conscience may doubt it.
>
> DANFORTH. Mr. Hale, you surely do not doubt my justice.
>
> HALE. I have this morning signed away the soul of Rebecca Nurse, Your Honor. I'll not conceal it, my hand shakes yet as with a wound!

THE HISTORICAL REBECCA NURSE AND JOHN PROCTOR

At first, the witches who were brought to trial and convicted were generally old and eccentric women like Sarah Good who were of questionable character long before the trials began. But people like Rebecca Nurse and John Proctor were not. As Miller has Parris say to Judge Hathorne in Act Four: "it were another sort that hanged till now. Rebecca Nurse is no Bridget that lived three year with Bishop before she married him. John Proctor is not Isaac Ward that drank his family to ruin." In late June, Rebecca Nurse was found guilty and sentenced to hang after an earlier verdict of "not guilty" was curiously reversed. Her minister, the Reverend Nicholas Noyes again, decided along with his congregation that she should be excommunicated for the good of the church. Miller seems to have been especially moved by her character and her almost unbelievable trial and conviction, as he indicates by his comments in the "Introduction" and his interpolated remarks in Act One. On Tuesday, July 19, 1692, she was hanged on Gallows Hill along with four others, all women. She was seventy-one years old. After the hanging, according to [American author and historian, Marion L.] Starkey:

> The bodies of the witches were thrust into a shallow grave in a crevice of Gallows Hill's outcropping of felsite. But the body of Rebecca did not remain there. Her children bided their time . . . and at night when the crowds and the executioners had gone home again, they gathered up the body of their mother and took it home. Just where they laid it none can know, for this was a secret thing and not even Parris, whose parsonage was not a quarter of a mile up the road past the grove where the Nurses buried their dead, must see that a new grave had been opened and prayers said. This was the hour

and the power of darkness when a son could not say where he had buried his mother.

Historically, Proctor was even more of a victim of the laws of his time than Miller details in *The Crucible*. Although the real John Proctor fought against his arrest and conviction as fervently as anyone could under the circumstances, he, like Miller's Proctor, was adamant in his refusal to confess to witchcraft because he did not believe it existed. And although fifty-two of his friends and neighbors risked their own safety to sign a petition in his behalf, nothing was done to re-examine the evidence against him. Ironically, Proctor's wife—in whose interest he had originally become involved in the affair—had become pregnant and, although sentenced, would never hang. She was eventually released after enduring her husband's public execution, the birth of her child in prison, and the seizure and loss of all her possessions.

Under the law, the goods and property of witches could be confiscated after their trial and conviction. In Proctor's case, however, the sheriff did not wait for the trial or the conviction. A contemporary account of the seizure indicates that neither Proctor nor his wife were ever expected to return from prison:

> John Proctor and his Wife being in Prison, the Sheriff came to his House and seized all the Goods, Provisions, and Cattle that he could come at, and sold some of the Cattle at half price, and killed others, and put them up for the West-Indies; threw out the Beer out of a Barrel, and carried away the Barrel; emptied a Pot of Broath, and took away the Pot, and left nothing in the House for the support of the Children: No part of the said Goods are known to be returned.

(The Proctors had five children, the youngest of whom were three and seven.) Along with three other men and one woman, John Proctor was hanged on August 19. On September 22, seven more witches and one wizard were hanged, and then the executions suddenly ended.

THE JUDGES AT SALEM

Miller has symbolized all the judges of the witchcraft trials in the figures of Danforth and Hathorne (Nathaniel Hawthorne's ancestor), and presented them as being more "official" in a legal sense than their historical models actually were. None of the judges in the trials had any legal training, and, apparently, neither had anyone else who was administering the law in the Massachusetts Bay Colony. According to

Starkey, the curious nature of the trials was in part due to the Puritans' limited understanding of the law, their contempt for lawyers, and their nearly total reliance on the Bible as a guide for all matters of legal and moral authority:

> The Puritans had a low opinion of lawyers and did not permit the professional practice of law in the colony. In effect the administration of the law was in the hands of laymen, most of them second-generation colonists who had an incomplete grasp of current principles of English jurisdiction. For that matter, this chosen people, this community which submitted itself to the direct rule of God, looked less to England for its precepts than to God's ancient and holy word. So far as was practicable the Puritans were living by a legal system that antedated the Magna Carta by at least two millennia, the Decalogue and the tribal laws codified in the Pentateuch.

As historians occasionally have pointed out, the executions did not stop because the people in Massachusetts suddenly ceased to believe in either the Devil or witchcraft; they stopped, simply and ironically, because of a legal question. There never was any doubt for most people living in New England in 1692 whether or not witchcraft was real or whether witches should be executed; the question centered around the reliability of spectral evidence coming from the testimony of the afflicted. It was largely through the determinations of Increase Mather and fourteen other Boston ministers that such testimony was declared to be insufficient for conviction and therefore became inadmissable as evidence. It was better, they concluded, to allow ten witches to escape than to hang one innocent person. In late October, Governor Phips officially dismissed the Court of Oyer and Terminer, and— although the trials continued through the following April—in May, 1693 he issued a proclamation discharging all the remaining "witches" and pardoning those who had fled the colony rather than face arrest, trial, and certain conviction.

Miller has said that if he were to rewrite *The Crucible*, he would make an open thematic issue of the evil he now believes to be represented by the Salem judges. His altered viewpoint toward the play may be accounted for partially as a reconsideration of his intensive examination of the trial records which, he has said, do not "reveal any mitigation of the unrelieved, straightforward, and absolute dedication to evil displayed by the judges of these trials and the prosecutors. After days of study it became quite incredible how perfect they were in this respect."

Miller's subsequent view of evil, however, did not come entirely from his study of the trial records. Between writing *The Crucible* in 1952 and producing the "Introduction" to the *Collected Plays* in 1957, he underwent a personal crucible when he appeared before the House Un-American Activities Committee in 1956. Although the experience was understandably not without its effect on his later attitude toward Congressional "witchhunters," it should, nevertheless, be considered in relation to his comments on the judges and evil quoted above. A more accurate reflection of Miller's attitude while writing *The Crucible* appears perhaps most clearly in the account published in February, 1953 of his thoughts while standing on the rock at Gallows Hill:

> Here hung Rebecca, John Proctor, George Jacobs—people more real to me than the living can ever be. The sense of a terrible marvel again; that people could have such a belief in themselves and in the rightness of their consciences as to give their lives rather than say what they thought was false. Or, perhaps, they only feared Hell so much? Yet, Rebecca said, and it is written in the record, "I cannot belie myself." And she knew it would kill her. . . . The rock stands forever in Salem. They knew who they were. Nineteen.

Like the rock at Salem, *The Crucible* has endured beyond the immediate events of its own time. If it was originally seen as a political allegory, it is presently seen by contemporary audiences almost entirely as a distinguished American play by an equally distinguished American playwright. As one of the most frequently produced plays in the American theater, *The Crucible* has attained a life of its own; one that both interprets and defines the cultural and historical background of American society. Given the general lack of plays in the American theater that have seriously undertaken to explore the meaning and significance of the American past in relation to the present, *The Crucible* stands virtually alone as a dramatically coherent rendition of one of the most terrifying chapters in American history.

Miller Twists Historical Fact to Present a Weak Allegory

Robert Warshow

Reviewing the first production of *The Crucible*, Robert Warshow charges that the play lacks substance and is based on false liberal assumptions. For example, the premise that the Salem witch trials were political is false because the trials were not a matter of civil rights but the manifestation of an errant metaphysical, religious view of the world. Warshow criticizes the play for its simplistic characters, arguing that they lack both religious and psychological complexity, and dismisses Proctor's motive, his guilt stemming from adultery, as a convenient theatrical convention. Similarly, Warshow claims that Miller reduces the complexities of history and experience to a few simple ideas, failing to offer particular insights and truths and rendering any message undecipherable. He builds the argument that the liberal Miller is conspiring with a liberal theater audience to celebrate a dramatic experience void of content.

Robert Warshow was an associate editor of *Commentary*.

One of the things that have been said of *The Crucible*, Arthur Miller's new play about the Salem witchcraft trials, is that we must not be misled by its obvious contemporary relevance: it is a drama of universal significance. This statement, which has usually a somewhat apologetic tone, seems to be made most often by those who do not fail to place great stress on the play's "timeliness." I believe it means something very different from what it appears to say, almost the contrary, in fact, and yet not quite the contrary

Excerpted from "The Liberal Conscience and *The Crucible*," by Robert Warshow, *Commentary*, March 1953. Reprinted by permission; all rights reserved.

either. It means: do not be misled by the play's historical theme into forgetting the main point, which is that "witch trials" are always with us, and especially today; but on the other hand do not hold Mr. Miller responsible either for the inadequacies of his presentation of the Salem trials or for the many undeniable and important differences between those trials and the "witch trials" that are going on now. It is quite true, nevertheless, that the play is, at least in one sense, of "universal significance." Only we must ask what this phrase has come to mean, and whether the quality it denotes is a virtue. . . .

MILLER'S INTERPRETATION OF THE SALEM TRIALS

The Salem witch trials represent how far the Puritans were ready to go in taking their doctrines seriously. Leaving aside the slavery question and what has flowed from it, those trials are perhaps the most disconcerting single episode in our history: the occurrence of the unthinkable on American soil, and in what our schools have rather successfully taught us to think of as the very "cradle of Americanism." Of Europe's witch trials, we have our opinion. But these witch trials are "ours"; where do they belong in the "tradition"?

For Americans, a problem of this sort demands to be resolved, and there have been two main ways of resolving it. The first is to regard the trials as a historical curiosity; a curiosity by definition requires no explanation. In this way the trials are placed among the "vagaries" of the Puritan mind and can even offer a kind of amusement, like the amusement we have surprisingly agreed to find in the so-called "rough justice" of the Western frontier in the last century. But the more usual and more deceptive way of dealing with the Salem trials has been to assimilate them to the history of progress in civil rights. This brings them into the world of politics, where, even if our minds are not always made up, at least we think we know what the issues are. Arthur Miller, I need hardly say, has adopted this latter view.

Inevitably, I suppose, we will find in history what we need to find. But in this particular "interpretation" of the facts there seems to be a special injustice. The Salem trials were not political and had nothing whatever to do with civil rights, unless it is a violation of civil rights to hang a murderer. Nor were the "witches" being "persecuted"—as the

Puritans did persecute Quakers, for instance. The actual conduct of the trials, to be sure, was outrageous, but no more outrageous than the conduct of ordinary criminal trials in England at the time. In any case, it is a little absurd to make the whole matter rest on the question of fair trial: how can there be a "fair trial" for a crime which not only has not been committed, but is impossible? The Salem "witches" suffered something that may be worse than persecution: they were hanged because of a metaphysical error. And they chose to die—for all could have saved themselves by "confession"—not for a cause, not for "civil rights," not even to defeat the error that hanged them, but for their own credit on earth and in heaven: they would not say they were witches when they were not. They lived in a universe where each man was saved or damned by himself, and what happened to them was personal. Certainly their fate is not lacking in universal significance; it was a human fate. But its universality—if we must have the word—is of that true kind which begins and ends in a time and a place. One need not believe in witches, or even in God, to understand the events in Salem, but it is mere provinciality to ignore the fact that both those ideas had a reality for the people of Salem that they do not have for us.

LIMITED CHARACTERIZATION IN *THE CRUCIBLE*

The "universality" of Mr. Miller's play belongs neither to literature nor to history, but to that journalism of limp erudition which assumes that events are to be understood by referring them to categories, and which is therefore never at a loss for a comment. Just as in *Death of a Salesman* Mr. Miller sought to present "the American" by eliminating so far as possible the "non-essential" facts which might have made his protagonist a particular American, so in *The Crucible* he reveals at every turn his almost contemptuous lack of interest in the particularities—which is to say, the reality— of the Salem trials. The character and motives of all the actors in this drama are for him both simple and clear. The girls who raised the accusation of witchcraft were merely trying to cover up their own misbehavior. The Reverend Samuel Parris found in the investigation of witchcraft a convenient means of consolidating his shaky position in a parish that was murmuring against his "undemocratic" conduct of the church. The Reverend John Hale, a conscientious and troubled minister who, given the premises, must have represented something like the best that Puritan New England had to offer, and whose agonies of doubt might have been expected to call forth the highest talents of a serious playwright, appears in *The Crucible* as a kind of idiotic "liberal" scoutmaster, at first cheerfully confident of his ability to cope with the Devil's wiles and in the last act babbling hysterically in an almost comic contrast to the assured dignity of the main characters. Deputy Governor Danforth, presented as the virtual embodiment of early New England, never becomes more than a pompous, unimaginative politician of the better sort.

As for the victims themselves, the most significant fact is Miller's choice of John Proctor for his leading character: Proctor can be seen as one of the more "modern" figures in the trials, hardheaded, skeptical, a voice of common sense (he thought the accusing girls could be cured of their "spells" by a sound whipping); also, according to Mr. Miller, no great churchgoer. It is all too easy to make Proctor into the "common man"—and then, of course, we know where we are: Proctor wavers a good deal, fails to understand what is happening, wants only to be left alone with his wife and his farm, considers making a false confession, but in the end goes to his death for reasons that he finds a little hard to define but that are clearly good reasons—mainly, it seems, he does not want to implicate others. You will never learn from this John Proctor that Salem was a religious community, quite as ready to hang a Quaker as a witch. The saintly Rebecca Nurse is also there, to be sure, sketched in rapidly in the background, a quiet figure whose mere presence—there is little more of her than that—reminds us how far the dramatist has fallen short.

Nor has Mr. Miller hesitated to alter the facts to fit his constricted field of vision. Abigail Williams, one of the chief accusers in the trials, was about eleven years old in 1692; Miller makes her a young woman of eighteen or nineteen and invents an adulterous relation between her and John Proctor in order to motivate her denunciation of John and his wife Elizabeth. The point is not that this falsifies the facts of Proctor's life (though one remembers uneasily that he himself was willing to be hanged rather than confess to what was not true), but that it destroys the play, offering an easy theatrical motive that even in theatrical terms explains nothing, and deliberately casting away the element of religious and psychological complexity which gives the Salem trials their dramatic interest in the first place. In a similar way, Miller risks the whole point of *Death of a Salesman* by making his plot turn on the irrelevant discovery of Willy Loman's adultery. And in both plays the fact of adultery itself is slighted: it is brought in not as a human problem, but as a mere theatrical device, like the dropping of a letter; one cannot take an interest in Willy Loman's philandering, or believe in Abigail Williams' passion despite the barnyard analogies with which the playwright tries to make it "elemental."

MILLER'S LACK OF INTELLECTUAL COMPLEXITY

Mr. Miller's steadfast, one might almost say selfless, refusal of complexity, the assured simplicity of his view of human behavior, may be the chief source of his ability to captivate the educated audience. He is an oddly depersonalized writer; one tries in vain to define his special quality, only to discover that it is perhaps not a quality at all, but something like a method, and even as a method strangely bare: his plays are as neatly put together and essentially as empty as that skeleton of a house which made *Death of a Salesman* so impressively confusing. He is the playwright of an audience that believes the frightening complexities of history and experience are to be met with a few ideas, and yet does not even possess these ideas any longer but can only point significantly at the place where they were last seen and where it is hoped they might still be found to exist. What this audience demands of its artists above all is an intelligent narrowness of mind and vision and a generalized tone of affirmation, offering not any particular insights or any particular truths, but simply the assurance that insight and truth as qualities, the things in themselves, reside somehow in the various signals by which the artist and the audience have learned to recognize each other. For indeed very little remains except this recognition; the marriage of the liberal theater and the liberal audience has been for some time a marriage in name only, held together by habit and mutual interest, partly by sentimental memory, most of all by the fear of loneliness and the outside world; and yet the movements of love are still kept up—for the sake of the children, perhaps.

The hero of this audience is Clifford Odets.[1] Among those who shouted "Bravo!" at the end of *The Crucible*—an exclama-

1. American playwright

tion, awkward on American lips, that is reserved for cultural achievements of the greatest importance—there must surely have been some who had stood up to shout "Strike!" at the end of *Waiting for Lefty.* But it is hard to believe that a second Odets, if that were possible, or the old Odets restored to youth, would be greeted with such enthusiasm as Arthur Miller calls forth. Odets's talent was too rich—in my opinion the richest ever to appear in the American theater—and his poetry and invention were constantly more important than what he conceived himself to be saying. In those days it didn't matter: the "message" at the end of the third act was so much taken for granted that there was room for Odets's exuberance, and he himself was never forced to learn how much his talent was superior to his "affirmations" (if he had learned, perhaps the talent might have survived the "affirmations"). Arthur Miller is the dramatist of a later time, when the "message" isn't there at all, but it has been agreed to pretend that it is. This pretense can be maintained only by the most rigid control, for there is no telling what small element of dramatic *élan* or simple reality may destroy the delicate rapport of a theater and an audience that have not yet acknowledged they have no more to say to each other. Arthur Miller is Odets without the poetry. Worst of all, one feels sometimes that he has suppressed the poetry deliberately, making himself by choice the anonymous dramatist of a fossilized audience. In *Death of a Salesman,* certainly, there were moments when reality seemed to force its way momentarily to the surface. And even at *The Crucible*—though here it was not Miller's suppressed talent that broke through, but the suppressed facts of the outside world—the thread that tied the audience to its dramatist must have been now and then under some strain: surely there were some in the audience to notice uneasily that these witch trials, with their quality of ritual and their insistent need for "confessions," were much more like the trial that had just ended in Prague than like any trial that has lately taken place in the United States. So much the better, perhaps, for the play's "universal significance"; I don't suppose Mr. Miller would defend the Prague trial. And yet I cannot believe it was for this particular implication that anyone shouted "Bravo!"

THE PLAY'S LACK OF CONTENT

For let us indeed not be misled. Mr. Miller has nothing to say about the Salem trials and makes only the flimsiest pretense that he has. *The Crucible* was written to say something about Alger Hiss and Owen Lattimore, Julius and Ethel Rosenberg, Senator McCarthy, the actors who have lost their jobs on radio and television, in short the whole complex that is spoken of, with a certain lowering of the voice, as the "present atmosphere." And yet not to say anything about that either, but only to suggest that a great deal might be said, oh an infinitely great deal, if it were not that—what? Well, perhaps if it were not that the "present atmosphere" itself makes such plain speaking impossible. As it is, there is nothing for it but to write plays of "universal significance"—and, after all, that's what a serious dramatist is supposed to do anyway.

What, then, *is* Mr. Miller trying to say to us? It's hard to tell. In *The Crucible* innocent people are accused and convicted of witchcraft on the most absurd testimony—in fact, the testimony of those who themselves have meddled in witchcraft and are therefore doubly to be distrusted. Decent citizens who sign petitions attesting to the good character of their accused friends and neighbors are thrown into prison as suspects. Anyone who tries to introduce into court the voice of reason is likely to be held in contempt. One of the accused refuses to plead and is pressed to death. No one is acquitted; the only way out for the accused is to make false confessions and themselves join the accusers. Seeing all this on the stage, we are free to reflect that something very like these trials has been going on in recent years in the United States. How much like? Mr. Miller does not say. But *very* like, allowing of course for some superficial differences: no one has been pressed to death in recent years, for instance. Still, people have lost their jobs for refusing to say under oath whether or not they are Communists. The essential pattern is the same, isn't it? And when we speak of "universal significance," we mean sticking to the essential pattern, don't we? Mr. Miller is under no obligation to tell us whether he thinks the trial of Alger Hiss, let us say, was a "witch trial"; he is writing about the Salem trials.

Or, again, the play reaches its climax with John and Elizabeth Proctor facing the problem of whether John should save himself from execution by making a false confession; he elects finally to accept death, for his tormentors will not be satisfied with his mere admission of guilt: he would be required to implicate others, thus betraying his innocent

friends, and his confession would of course be used to justify the hanging of the other convicted witches in the face of
growing community unrest. Now it is very hard to watch
this scene without thinking of Julius and Ethel Rosenberg,
who might also save their lives by confessing. Does Mr.
Miller believe that the only confession possible for them
would be a false one, implicating innocent people? Natu-
rally, there is no way for him to let us know; perhaps he was
not even thinking of the Rosenbergs at all. How can he be
held responsible for what comes into my head while I
watch his play? And if I think of the Rosenbergs and somebody else thinks of Alger Hiss, and still another thinks of the
Prague trial, doesn't that simply prove all over again that the
play has universal significance?

One remembers also, as John Proctor wrestles with his
conscience, that a former close associate of Mr. Miller's decided some time ago, no doubt after serious and painful
consideration, to tell the truth about his past membership in
the Communist party, that he mentioned some others who
had been in the party with him, and that he then became
known in certain theatrical circles as an "informer" and a
"rat." Is it possible that this is what Mr. Miller was thinking
about when he came to write his last scene? And is he trying to tell us that no one who has been a member of the
Communist party should admit it? Or that if he does admit
it he should not implicate anyone else? Or that all such
"confessions" may be assumed to be false? If he were trying
to tell us any of these things, perhaps we might have some
arguments to raise. But of course he isn't; he's only writing
about the Salem trials, and who wants to maintain that John
Proctor was guilty of witchcraft?

But if Mr. Miller isn't saying anything about the Salem
trials, and can't be caught saying anything about anything
else, what did the audience think he was saying? That too is
hard to tell. A couple of the newspaper critics wrote about
how timely the play was, and then took it back in the Sunday editions, putting a little more weight on the "universal
significance"; but perhaps they didn't quite take it back as
much as they seemed to want to: the final verdict appeared
to be merely that *The Crucible* is not so great a play as *Death
of a Salesman*. As for the rest of the audience, it was clear
that they felt themselves to be participating in an event of
great meaning: that is what is meant by "Bravo!" Does

"Bravo!" mean anything else? I think it means: we agree with Arthur Miller; he has set forth brilliantly and courageously what has been weighing on all our minds; at last someone has had the courage to answer Senator McCarthy.

I don't believe this audience was likely to ask itself what it was agreeing to. Enough that someone had said something, anything, to dispel for a couple of hours that undefined but very real sense of frustration which oppresses these "liberals"—who believe in their innermost being that salvation comes from saying something, and who yet find themselves somehow without anything very relevant to say. They tell themselves, of course, that Senator McCarthy has made it "impossible" to speak; but one can hardly believe they are satisfied with this explanation. Where are the heroic voices that will refuse to be stilled?

Well, last season there was *The Male Animal,* a play written twelve or thirteen years ago about a college professor who gets in trouble for reading one of Vanzetti's[2] letters to his English composition class. In the audience at that play one felt also the sense of communal excitement; it was a little like a secret meeting of early Christians—or even, one might say, witches—where everything had an extra dimension of meaning experienced only by the communicants. And this year there has been a revival of *The Children's Hour,* a play of even more universal significance than *The Crucible* since it doesn't have anything to do with any trials but just shows how people can be hurt by having lies told about them. But these were old plays, the voices of an older generation. It remained for Arthur Miller to write a new play that really speaks out.

What does he say when he speaks out?

Never mind. He speaks out. . . .

MILLER'S LIBERAL AUDIENCE

In however inchoate a fashion, those who sat thrilled in the dark theater watching *The Crucible* were celebrating a tradition and a community. No longer could they find any meaning in the cry of "Strike!" or "Revolt!" as they had done in their younger and more "primitive" age; let it be only "Bravo!"—a cry of celebration with no particular content. The important thing was that for a short time they could ex-

2. twentieth-century executed anarchist Bartolomeo

perience together the sense of their own being, their close community of right-mindedness in the orthodoxy of "dissent." Outside, there waited all kinds of agonizing and concrete problems: were the Rosenbergs actually guilty? was Stalin actually going to persecute the Jews? But in the theater they could know, immediately and confidently, their own innate and inalienable rightness.

The Salem trials are in fact more relevant than Arthur Miller can have suspected. For this community of "dissent," inexorably stripped of all principle and all specific belief, has retreated at last into a kind of extreme Calvinism of its own where political truth ceases to have any real connection with politics but becomes a property of the soul. Apart from all belief and all action, these people are "right" in themselves, and no longer need to prove themselves in the world of experience; the Revolution—or "liberalism," or "dissent"—has entered into them as the grace of God was once conceived to have entered into the "elect," and, like the grace of God, it is given irrevocably. Just as Alger Hiss bears witness to virtue even in his refusal to admit the very act wherein his "virtue" must reside if it resides anywhere, so those bear witness to "dissent" and "progress" in their mere existence.

For the Puritans themselves, the doctrine of absolute election was finally intolerable, and it cannot be believed that this new community of the elect finds its position comfortable. But it has yet to discover that its discomfort, like its "election," comes from within.

CHAPTER 2

Characterization and Themes in *The Crucible*

READINGS ON
THE CRUCIBLE

Major Characters in *The Crucible*

Edward Murray

Edward Murray identifies the rich personality traits of the major characters in *The Crucible*. According to Murray, John Proctor is physically powerful, distrustful of authority, and strong willed. Struggling against his own fears and guilt, reshaped by a new understanding of self at the end of the play, Proctor is a traditional tragic hero who gives voice to the transformation going on within him. Elizabeth Proctor's traits include sensitivity, pride, and slowness to forgive. Murray suggests that Elizabeth ultimately finds humility. Unlike the Proctors, Abigail does not grow in character. Throughout the play she remains commanding, dangerous, vain, and sexually passionate.

Murray writes that all of the leading characters are neatly linked to particular moral stances: John, for example, chooses principle; Elizabeth opts for John's goodness; Danforth is unyielding; and Abigail is self-seeking. Murray stresses, however, that *The Crucible* is not a simple morality play because the characters are interwoven with complex dramatic themes.

Edward Murray is a professor of English at State University of New York College at Brockport. His works include *Clifford Odets: The Thirties and After, Ten Film Classics,* and *The Cinematic Imagination: Writers and the Motion Pictures.* Murray is a contributor to *College Language Association Journal* and *Literature/Film Quarterly.*

The main characters in *Crucible*, contrary to some critical reports, are far from flat. John Proctor is described as a "farmer in his middle thirties," "powerful of body." In his first scene, John reveals himself as a man with a strong personality: "Abigail has stood as though on tiptoe, absorbing his presence, wide-eyed," while the other girl is "strangely titillated." That Abigail is willing to murder in order to possess John invests this farmer with a sense of importance. That John lusted with the girl in the past—against the law of God and Salem—reveals a certain daring in the man. That John has the will power to resist Abigail now, even while part of him still desires her, shows determination. Repeatedly, John displays his dislike of authoritarianism.

In Act Two, John makes a determined effort to please Elizabeth. He kisses her perfunctorily; he lies in saying that her cooking is well-seasoned (perhaps a kind of irony on the lack of spice in Elizabeth?). John seems motivated by guilt feelings in this scene. When Elizabeth urges him to go to court and expose Abigail, he is afraid that his relations with the girl will be brought to light. The question of whether the court will believe him would seem of secondary importance. The cardinal point is that John must struggle against his own fear. Miller attempts to integrate the "personal" and the "social" in a number of ways. "I cannot speak but I am doubted," says John, ". . . as though I come into a court when I come into this house!" Although John lies to Elizabeth about being alone with Abigail in Parris's house, he persists in defending his honesty.

John continues to struggle, throughout Act Three, against both his inner contradictions and his outer antagonists. He reveals his resourcefulness in securing a deposition. He shows his persistence in extracting a confession from Mary. When the charge against Elizabeth is suspended, John does not falter—he concentrates his attack on the court for the sake of others. And when Abigail seems to be winning the struggle, John makes public confession of his "lechery."

In Act Four, John "is another man, bearded, filthy, his eyes misty as though webs had overgrown them." The physical transformation signals an inner change in John. "I have been thinking," he tells Elizabeth, "I would confess to them." After a few months in jail contemplating his death a change of appearance and attitude on John's part is credible. John defends himself by saying: "Spite only keeps me silent," "I want my life." However, John has not overcome his inner conflict; he hesitates to implicate others, he balks at signing the confession. Gradually, John moves to a position of final defiance of the court: "I have three children—how may I teach them to walk like men . . . and I sold my friends?"

JOHN PROCTOR'S AWARENESS

In a November 1973 interview, Arthur Miller explains to his interviewer, Robert Corrigan, that unlike Willy Loman in Death of a Salesman, *John Proctor has a clear understanding of the source of his problems. Excerpts from the interview are reprinted in* Conversations with Arthur Miller, *edited by Matthew C. Roudané.*

CORRIGAN: . . . It is interesting in your later work that you see people as being much more able to recognize their responsibilities.

MILLER: Because in later work, the work itself is less subjective. In *The Crucible* there is no question but that it is the social organization which is conveying the tragic. John Proctor wouldn't be in that jam except for the actions of some politicians. Hence, the level of consciousness is far higher in John Proctor than in earlier protagonists. I mean, he does announce what the problem is and what the issues are because the real social situation makes that possible. He can verbalize what Willie—or most of us—cannot because the enemy is indistinct. It is all around us and inside of us.

Matthew C. Roudané, ed., *Conversations with Arthur Miller.* Jackson: University Press of Mississippi, 1987.

The foregoing shows clearly that John is rich in traits; that there is continuous development of his character; and that there is adequate preparation for his revelation in the last act.

JOHN PROCTOR AS A TRAGIC HERO

No critic, as far as I know, has questioned John Proctor's status as a "tragic hero." The controversy over the "common man" versus the "traditional hero" (usually Aristotelian), occasioned by the fate of Willy Loman,[1] is absent from discussions of *Crucible*. Miller would seem to have provided Proctor with all the heroic attributes dear to the heart of "traditionalists." Miller himself says: "In *The Crucible* . . . the characters were special people who could give voice to the things that were inside them. . . . These people knew what was happening to them." Whether this increase in articulateness makes *Crucible* a more powerful dramatic piece than *Death of a Salesman* is arguable.

Dialogue, it should be noted, fails to illuminate John's past. Is this lack of background a serious failing in *Crucible?*

1. protagonist in Miller's *Death of a Salesman*

In *All My Sons,* lack of adequate character exposition impaired credibility; in *Salesman,* the revelation of Willy's past had a direct bearing on the present line of development. In *Crucible,* however, the past would not seem to be pertinent. Each play should be approached on its own merits. *Crucible* focuses on a specific situation, and the reader possesses all the necessary facts for believing in that situation. Nor should one conclude that, since John's final speeches sound too theatrical, the language in the play is not adequate. The various summaries presented in this chapter should indicate that preparation, especially foreshadowing of character development, is expertly handled. Miller, in a very subtle manner, uses key words to knit together the texture of action and theme. Note, for example, the recurrent use of the word "soft." In Act One, John tells Abigail: "Abby, I may think of you *softly* from time to time. . . ." (italics mine); in Act Two, Hale tells John: "there is a *softness* in your record, sir, a *softness*" (italics mine). Dialogue, moreover, suggests that behind John's denunciation of Parris lies a guilty conscience. Hale says that John has missed church services a good deal in the past seventeen months; since Abigail has been removed from Proctor's house for the past seven months, the inference is that the real reason for John's backsliding has not been expressed.

ELIZABETH'S CHARACTER TRAITS

Miller is even more sparing than usual in his physical description of Elizabeth; that is, not one word is uttered about her appearance. Nor, as was the case with John, is anything conveyed about her background. Nevertheless, Elizabeth has many traits and she grows throughout the play. She is sensitive: "It hurt my heart to strip her, poor rabbit"; here, of course, Elizabeth is a foil to the murderous Abigail. Elizabeth betrays a weakness in asserting herself against Mary Warren, a weakness which John brands a "fault." She is also proud, slow to forgive, and suspicious. Frequently, Elizabeth—who is "cold"—fails in charity. But she will lie for a loved one, and, since she learns humility, she is capable of change. Elizabeth's dominant motive is her yearning for John's undivided love. In Act Two, for instance, behind Elizabeth's self-righteous and intolerant posture, there is love for John. She proves this love in Act Three when she lies to save John's life. Elizabeth continues to grow in the last act.

"Her wrists," says Miller, "are linked by heavy chain. . . . Her clothes are dirty; her face is pale and gaunt." The trials have worked their effect on Elizabeth, too. Danforth, uncomprehending, sees in her "dry eyes" the "proof of [her] unnatural life." Alone with her husband, however, Elizabeth says:

> I have read my heart this three month John. . . . I have sins of my own to count. It need a cold wife to prompt lechery.

> John, I counted myself so plain, so poorly made, no honest love could come to me! Suspicion kissed you when I did; I never knew how I should say my love. It were a cold house I kept.

Since Elizabeth remains in character, her development in Act Four, as was the case with John, is logical and believable.

ABIGAIL'S CHARACTER TRAITS

Abigail is much less complex and interesting than either John or Elizabeth. She is described as "seventeen . . . a strikingly beautiful girl, an orphan, with an endless capacity for dissembling." Dialogue fails to disclose anything about Abigail's past. In the course of the play, however, she reveals several traits: she is supersensitive, sexually passionate, and mentally alert; she is commanding and vain; she is a thief; and throughout the play, she makes painfully evident that she is capable of murder. Abigail's dominant motive is to destroy Elizabeth and sleep with John. Abigail remains in character; but she does not grow.

The minor characters, with the exception of Hale, are flat and static. There is a question of Miller's economy here, and Miller himself was not unaware of the problem. In *All My Sons,* Miller seemed to have employed more characters than he needed for the furtherance of either action or theme. In *The Crucible,* in spite of the fact that there are at least twenty-one characters, the problem does not seem acute, for as was pointed out in the discussion of structure, Miller managed to keep the developing action in thematic focus. If the numerous characters, such as Marshall Herrick or Ezekiel Cheever, contribute very little, if anything, to action or theme, it is also true that they do nothing to impede or becloud action and theme. Some readers might find many of these secondary figures mere "scenery"; whether Miller might have profitably eliminated them entirely is an interesting, but hardly a burning, technical question.

Although the characters will be discussed again in the following section, it should be noted here that all the leading ones represent various shadings on a thematic spectrum. John wavers between principle and compromise, and chooses, finally, principle; Elizabeth opts for John's "goodness," no matter what he finally chooses; Abigail is completely self-seeking; so is Parris; Rebecca is a witness to principle above compromise or deceit; Danforth is similarly unyielding about the inviolability of principle; while Hale, who alone among the minor characters grows, would abandon principle for the sake of life. This schematic neatness suggests that *Crucible* is not to be evaluated by a narrow adherence to a realistic or naturalistic norm. In the *Theatre Arts* issue last cited, Miller says: "*The Crucible* is not more realistic but more theatrical than *Death of a Salesman.*" Yet it would be a serious error to leap to the other extreme and dismiss Miller's play as a mere oversimplified morality play. Miller himself, as I have suggested, invites the latter approach, but it is entirely possible that the playwright, no less than his hostile critics, has missed the very real thematic complexity that *is* in *The Crucible.*

The Heroism of John Proctor

Julie Adam

Julie Adam writes that John Proctor's refusal to save himself has several important dimensions: It preserves his integrity, expiates his sin of adultery, saves others, and weakens his persecutors. Proctor's dilemma is to save his own life and betray his beliefs or sacrifice his life and uphold his ideals. His choice is made easier when he realizes that a decision to save himself means that he must side with the forces of evil. Although Proctor is charged by the authorities, he really condemns himself, pushing his private guilt into public view. According to Adam, Proctor's motivation to act as he does is based more on an examination of himself and his own personal guilt than on a desire to make a large social gesture of martyrdom. Ultimately Proctor realizes that the only way to maintain his integrity and insist on his individuality is to choose death. Proctor's struggle has led him to a heightened awareness of self but, in the process, he must become a scapegoat for society.

Julie Adam is a lecturer in modern drama and effective writing at the University of Toronto, Canada.

The idea of martyrdom lends itself . . . to liberal-humanist interpretations of heroism and suffering. As Raymond Williams contends in *Modern Tragedy*, during the nineteenth century the identification of the hypocritical, false society as the enemy of the individual facilitated the transformation of the bourgeois hero-as-victim into the hero-as-rebel against the hostile society. It was also at this time that the figure of the 'liberal martyr' or 'the heroic liberator opposed and destroyed by a false society' emerged. He identifies John Proctor in *The Crucible* as a 'liberal martyr', both a victim of

society and a potential deliverer—through sacrificial death—
of its people. Raymond Williams' description of the 'liberal
martyr' is also appropriate for the saviour/sacrificial figure
who combines the traits of both victim and victor and is destroyed as he or she stages a profoundly anti-social and personal rebellion which has its social ramifications.

JOHN PROCTOR'S DUALITY

The Crucible (1953) embodies the duality of private and social
motivation and the inherent tension. Although John Proctor's
action serves a social cause—he sacrifices himself in order to
save others and to stage a protest against his persecutors—he
is driven essentially by the impulse to preserve his integrity
as well as by the need to expiate his sin. By showing how
mass hysteria feeds on private guilt and encourages private
vengeance under the guise of self-righteous public accusation, the play examines that point where social imperatives
impinge upon individual freedom.

A jilted lover accuses Proctor of witchcraft, a very real accusation in the context of seventeenth-century Salem, regard-
less of twentieth-century attitudes. A paranoid society has condemned Proctor, but he has also condemned himself. He may
not actually be guilty of witchcraft, but he does carry the burden of guilt for his adultery. In a number of Miller's plays, especially where adultery plays a central role, for example in
Death of a Salesman, After the Fall and *The Crucible,* personal
guilt is often externalized as public guilt, and social morality is
reflected in, and often equated with, individual morality. In a
lengthy . . . stage direction, Miller describes Proctor as

> a sinner, a sinner not only against the moral fashion of the
> time, but against his own vision of decent conduct. . . . Proc-
> tor, respected and even feared in Salem, has come to regard
> himself as a kind of fraud.

Proctor's trial by the community is subordinate to his tense
trial of conscience in a drama in which self-examination,
judgement and acceptance of responsibility during personal
and societal crisis play an important role.

JOHN PROCTOR'S DILEMMA

Proctor is faced with a dilemma: he can save his life if he
confesses and betrays others, or he can sacrifice his life to
his ideals. He struggles with his conscience and, knowing
that he is morally blemished by adultery, thinks he cannot

justify a proud sacrifice or a false heroism. He feels unworthy of his propensity for martyrdom: 'I cannot mount the gibbet like a saint. It is a fraud. I am not that man', he objects. After considerable self-examination, he is willing to renounce his beliefs, to confess to his sins. However, when he realizes that he is expected to give up his confession to public use, he protests: 'You will not use me! . . . It is no part of salvation that you should use me'. After having put his signature to the recantation, he asks for his name back:

> Because it is my name! Because I cannot have another in my life! Because I lie and sign myself to lies! Because I am not worth the dust on the feet of them that hang! How may I live without my name? I have given you my soul; leave me my name!

Proctor comes face to face with the machinations of the community as he realizes that in order to save his life, he must side with the forces of evil. It is then that he decides to doff his guilty conscience and stand up to his persecutors.

Throughout his critical writings, and especially in 'The Shadows of the Gods', Miller criticizes the narrow—usually psychological—focus of contemporary theatre. He calls for greater emphasis on ultimate causes rather than mere effects. The modern preoccupation with the psyche of the alienated, frustrated individual must necessarily result, he says, in an impoverished dramatic vision and a loss of poetic power. As a consequence, in the 'Introduction to the Collected Plays', he insists that for modern drama to be faithful to reality, it must embrace 'both determinism and the paradox of will', because the unfortunate split between the private and the public domains results in a typically modern paradoxical need to 'write of private persons privately and lift up their means of expression to a poetic—that is, a social—level'. The realistic mode—a consciously created style best suited to the presentation of family relations and to individual psychological characterization—is inherently prosaic; only the dramatization of social relations, of a conflict of forces, of larger truths of existence—expressed in anti-realistic, expressionist modes—has poetic potential. Miller believes that the contemporary playwright who explores only the private mask and loses sight of the public individual inevitably remains earth-bound, for

> the current quest after the poetic as poetic is fruitless. It is an attempt to make apples grow without growing trees. It is seeking poetry precisely where poetry is not: in the private

---

THE EVIL OF THE SALEM TRIAL JUDGES

In a 1958 conversation with Phillip Gelb first published in the Educational Theatre Journal, *Arthur Miller reflects that he did not make the judge in* The Crucible *evil enough.*

Believe me, I think now my mistake in *The Crucible* was that I didn't make the judge evil enough. I think I should have gone the whole hog. I should have shown him conspiring with the witnesses to take evidence, which he did, still being a deeply religious man, a man who could quote any part of the Bible at will, who prayed at every opportunity, and met, as is known, with the girls who were hysterical and fed them cues as to what they should testify to an hour hence. He did that; there were others who did that. It was cooked up from their point of view. The hysteria, however, was not cooked up from the point of view of the average person in Salem. He believed it. And the judge was a great actor; he could get himself into a froth and a frenzy knowing, at the same time, that he had manufactured the whole thing. And one of the judges ended up drunk and insane as a result of the conflicts aroused in his mind by the behavior of this other judge and by his own behavior. I am trying to deal with that now, to tell you the truth. I am trying to deal with it because I can't see the problem of will evolving fruitfully unless the existence of evil is taken into account.

Matthew C. Roudané, ed., *Conversations with Arthur Miller.* Jackson: University Press of Mississippi, 1987.

---

life viewed entirely within the bounds of the subjective, the area of sensation, or the bizarre and the erotic.

The truly poetic—here he differentiates between the genuinely poetic and the merely lyrical—must be born of a balance between the private and the public and be a dramatic presentation of the whole person.

JOHN PROCTOR'S MOTIVATION

In *The Crucible* Miller emphasizes Proctor's increasing awareness of the interaction between private and public masks and dramatizes the initially-reluctant acceptance of the heroic role and of the martyr's fate following the painful process of self-scrutiny. Central to the play is Miller's idea that at certain times in history, at 'sharp' times as Deputy Governor Danforth calls them, humanity perceives two irreconcilable opposites operating in the world. It is at such crucial mo-

ments in the life of the community, 'when an individual conscience . . . [is] all that . . . [can] keep a world from falling',
that the individual must make a clear choice. Through his
refusal to name names and betray others, Proctor defines
himself as a good man, perhaps the only sane man in an insane universe which has condemned him. He emerges from
the crucible of his conscience a changed man; his character . . . is 'tried in the fire'.

It is questionable whether Proctor's proud acceptance of
death partakes of the heroism Butcher[1] calls 'impersonal ar-
dour in the cause of right'. Although he selflessly refuses to
turn against his friends and neighbours, it is in fact his personal integrity that is at stake if he recants and confesses.
Proctor's motivation is individualistic rather than genuinely
social and akin to what Raymond Williams, in his *Modern
Tragedy*, calls 'personal verification by death'. Such diverse
characters as Rudolph (in *The Masque of Kings*), Essex and
Willy all verify their identity through death and share a sui-
cidal tendency which Williams considers to be 'the last stage
of liberal tragedy'.

JOHN PROCTOR'S INDIVIDUALISM

Miller, too, has pointed out that his ultimate concern was
with the assault on the identity of the individual in a socially
hostile situation. He

> wished for a way to write a play that would be sharp, that
> would lift out of the morass of subjectivism that squirming,
> single, defined process which would show that the sin of pub-
> lic terror is that it divests man of conscience of himself.

In Proctor's circumstances, the only means of regaining this
integrity is through death. Essentially all martyrs find themselves in a similar predicament. This play, like a number of
others, explores the possibility of maintaining individual integrity in an oppressive environment. Therefore, the outsider's private rebellion has public significance precisely because it is individualistic. That is, by insisting on their
individuality, martyr figures stage a protest against public
norms and expectations.

In a further development of liberal tragedy, the figure of
the martyr is often related to that of the scapegoat; indeed,
the hero may be presented as a persecuted outsider, a sacri-

1. literary critic S.H.

ficial victim of society and at the same time someone of
heightened sensibility and superior conscience who chooses
his or her fate. Northrup Frye suggests in *Anatomy of Criticism* that

> the figure of a typical or random victim begins to crystallize
> in domestic tragedy as it deepens in ironic tone. We may call
> this typical victim the *pharmakos* or scapegoat. We meet a
> *pharmakos* figure in Hawthorne's Hester Prynne, in Mel-
> ville's Billy Budd, in Hardy's Tess, in the Septimus of *Mrs.
> Dalloway*, in the stories of persecuted Jews and Negroes, in
> the stories of artists whose genius makes them Ishmaels of a
> bourgeois society. The *pharmakos* is neither innocent nor
> guilty. He is innocent in the sense that what happens to him
> is far greater than anything he has done provokes, like the
> mountaineer whose shout brings down an avalanche. He is
> guilty in the sense that he is a member of a guilty society, or
> living in a world where such injustices are an inescapable
> part of existence.

The ambivalence of guilt and the complexity of innocence
figure frequently in the plays of Eugene O'Neill, Miller and
Tennessee Williams where the characters' punishments far
exceed their crimes and where their existential unease is a
function of their complicity in a valueless world.

An Atmosphere of Dread in *The Crucible*

C.J. Partridge

C.J. Partridge discusses Miller's use of characterization to develop a sense of dread. As Betty lies afflicted, there is a mounting mood of apprehension in the Parris household. Partridge states that Reverend Parris fears the disorder that is entering his house, exemplified by his repeated use of the word "unnatural." When Mrs. Putnam enters, any hope that Parris had of maintaining order is lost. The fanatical Mrs. Putnam, hardened by the loss of seven children, announces the presence of the devil, initiating the onslaught of the disorder that will spread to the entire community.

Partridge describes Parris as an insecure and compromising authority whose weaknesses are heightened by a sense of persecution. He becomes dangerous when his mounting fear of conspiracies works to undermine his perceived authority and status. In contrast to Parris, Reverend Hale presents himself to the community as a scholarly, self-assured man. Partridge argues, however, that Hale's weakness is his unwillingness to question or challenge his fundamental assumptions. Parris's insecurity, Mrs. Putnam's fanaticism, and Hale's dangerous theological dogmatism are intensified by the common-sense Rebecca Nurse. Partridge concludes that the underlying flaws of the characters introduced in the early scenes create an atmosphere of dread that allows hysteria to infest Salem.

C.J. Partridge is an assistant professor in the Department of English at the University of Victoria, B.C., Canada. His writings include *Minor American Fiction, 1920–1940: A Survey and an Introduction, Death of a Salesman: A. Miller,* and *Coriolanus: Shakespeare.*

Although *The Crucible* should never be seen as a mechanical parable about McCarthyite America, the atmosphere of dread in the Salem of 1692 may be paralleled with the world of the

Reprinted from *The Crucible (Arthur Miller)*, by C.J. Partridge, Notes on English Literature (Oxford: Blackwell, 1971), by permission of the author.

late nineteen-forties and early nineteen-fifties. We . . . shall now examine in detail the manner in which Miller drama-tizes a mood of fear and repression.

All the names used in *The Crucible* are authentic, as are the fates of the persons. However, as little is really known of the villagers' lives or temperaments, the characters behind the names have been 'rounded out' by Miller's dramatic imagination.

DISORDER INVADES SALEM

The spring of 1692 did not produce an awareness of new life or new vigour for the inhabitants of Salem. In the opening scene the morning sunlight streams through a narrow win-dow in the Reverend Parris's house. It casts only a small light into a room of sparse austerity. Although objects are carefully arranged about the room, suggesting a clerical order and self-discipline, a contrast between light and dark is immedi-ately conveyed to a spectator. The middle-aged minister prays against the dark sickness which afflicts his daughter. He is distraught at a sense of disorder which he fears is entering his home. His peremptory dismissal of the black slave Tituba and his semi-coherent prayers dramatize, by broken phrases and abrupt rhythms, both the pain in his mind and the omi-nous invading disorder

The entry of Susanna Walcott—nervously, hurriedly—adds to these implications of disruption. She has come direct from Doctor Griggs; the physician is reported as advising—in the manner the court records report the historical Doctor Griggs—that the father 'might look to unnatural things for the cause' of his daughter's sickness. Parris is further pained at the suggestion, repeating the word 'unnatural' several times, thus setting up, as it were, ominous reverberations in the mind of a spectator.

Parris has reason to be apprehensive. He knows his daughter Betty, his adopted niece Abigail Williams and his slave Tituba, all members of his 'orderly' household, have danced at night in the forest—in the popular imagination that 'disorderly' domain of the devil. Now, as Abigail tells him, 'the rumour of witchcraft is all about' and Parris fears that enemies in the parish may conspire to remove him from his ministry.

Unfortunately, his fears are compounded with the appear-ance of Mrs. Putnam. She bursts into the room, breaking apart the slender restoration of order which Parris has been trying to achieve through his conversations with Susanna Walcott and Abigail Williams. Mrs. Putnam enters as a positive force, convinced of diabolical malevolence in the community. Her first words are aimed directly at the minister:

> MRS. PUTNAM (*full of breath, shiny-eyed*): It is a marvel. It is surely a stroke of hell upon you.
>
> PARRIS: No, Goody Putnam, it is—
>
> MRS. PUTNAM (*glancing at Betty*): How high did she fly, how high?
>
> PARRIS: No, no, she never flew—

The imagery she uses in her following comments conveys both her own conviction of the devil's presence and the positive incursion of disorder into the 'clean spareness' of the Puritan community. The Reverend Parris's daughter, she asserts, has been seen flying over a barn and alighting like a bird. Her own daughter, Ruth, is also sick; but 'with vicious certainty' she states that this is no natural sickness:

> I'd not call it sick: the Devil's touch is heavier than sick. It's death, y'know, it's death drivin' into them, forked and hoofed.

Parris's self-assurance dwindles before the certainty of Mrs. Putnam and her husband. Already he begins to assume a defensive posture, almost pleading with Thomas Putnam not to assert the presence of unnatural elements:

> Thomas, Thomas, I pray you, leap not to witchcraft. I know that you—you least of all, Thomas, would ever wish so disastrous a charge laid upon me. We cannot leap to witchcraft. They will howl me out of Salem for such corruption in my house.

The minister's tone of intense pleading is the more understandable when it is realized that Thomas Putnam has been one of his main supporters in the village. When disagreements broke out, Thomas Putnam sided with him and Parris knows his indebtedness to, and reliance on, this influential man of the parish.

THE FANATICISM OF THE PUTNAMS

The Putnams are a strange couple. Thomas is wealthy but seems to have an obsession with influencing other people and hence making his will prevail in the community. He continually intrigues over land, seeking to increase his already large holdings but, ironically, of the couple's eight children seven have died. Now the surviving child, Ruth, is sick. There is consequently the possibility of no heir to the family fortune. Mrs. Putnam is desperate. She is convinced that unnatural forces have caused the deaths of her children. In her desperation she has sent Ruth to Tituba who, it is thought, can speak with the dead to learn who has murdered all her offspring. It was a curious recourse for this forty-five-year-old Christian woman to seek help from the pagan (obeah) beliefs of a West Indian slave.

The first impression of Ann Putnam on a spectator can only be unsympathetic. The imagery suggestive of witchcraft and devilry which marks her initial appearance conveys her outer hardness of assertion and fanatical conviction. But there is a terrible pathos behind this outer hardness—a pathos which is revealed by her words to the minister when she relates the misfortunes attending her children:

> I have laid seven babies unbaptized in the earth. Believe me, sir, you never saw more hearty babies born. And yet, each would wither in my arms the very night of their birth. I have spoke nothin' but my heart has clamoured intimations. And now, this year, my Ruth, my only—I see her turning strange. A secret child she has become this year, and shrivels like a sucking mouth were pullin' on her life too. And so I thought to send her to your Tituba—

The simple language and cadenced phrases, like the gasp of a woman whose life has become one long sob, beautifully express the frustrated tenderness of a mother deprived of giving love to her children.

REVEREND PARRIS'S INSECURITY

With the Putnams' accusations that witches are at work murdering members of the community, Reverend Parris feels a 'frantic terror': there is an imputation that Tituba and possibly Abigail are involved. Putnam encourages him to proclaim publicly the discovery of witchcraft. Parris is swayed but seeks a temporary compromise; he will lead the villagers in a psalm, but will not yet announce the presence of witches.

As his character is revealed through the events of Act One, he is shown as a man with a basic insecurity. This tends to make him compromising and subservient before men of influence such as Putnam. When criticized by social inferiors among his parishioners, however, his essential insecurity makes him emphasize his status and clerical rights; material goods are the outward expression of his status and Parris has been prepared to squabble over his salary and provision of firewood, and to demand the deed of the house in which he lives. His insecurity is heightened by a sense of persecution— a faction conspiring against him—and, as a man possessing unsure authority, he exaggerates the role of authority in the community. Preaching 'hellfire and bloody damnation', he asserts: 'There is either obedience or the church will burn like Hell is burning!'

The insecurity of such a nature may become a dangerous thing when it is felt that conspiracies are growing on all sides to undermine one's status and authority. Parris exclaims:

> You will look far for a man of my kind at sixty pound a year! I am not used to this poverty; I left a thrifty business in the Barbados to serve the Lord. I do not fathom it, why am I persecuted here? I cannot offer one proposition but there be a howling riot of argument. I have often wondered if the Devil be in it somewhere; I cannot understand you people otherwise

Such petulance assumes ominous overtones when, like Dr. Griggs, Reverend Parris is readily willing to ascribe 'unnatural' and diabolical causes to human activities.

THE PRETENTIOUSNESS OF REVEREND HALE

In contrast to Parris's profound insecurity, Reverend John Hale enters the village of Salem and the Parris household with all the assurance that learning, and a reputation for learning, can provide. He is anxious to be of service. Insecurity may be the foundation of the Reverend Parris's appeals to authority: a whole edifice of knowledge is to be placed by the Reverend Hale at the service of the villagers.

But there is a defect in the type of learning and the mentality which Hale embodies. Despite vast quantities of thought and reading, his mind has failed to question the fundamental assumptions on which it rests. Reverend Hale has never questioned, for instance, the reality of the devil; upon the assumption that the devil exists and is always seeking to extend his malignant power, he has built his intellectual edifice. His knowledge supports an existing theological or ideological structure; it does not question that structure. Miller reminds us that in contemporary societies a communist intellectual may similarly never question the malignancy of capitalism, or an intellectual in Western Europe or North America may too rarely question the reputed evils of communism. As a consequence learning, no matter how vast and impressive, having failed to be sceptical of basic assumptions, can easily appear hollow and pretentious. Such is the effect of Reverend Hale's learning—an effect made on his first appearance.

Miller describes him as being like 'a young doctor on his first call. His painfully acquired armoury of symptoms, catch-words, and diagnostic procedures are now to be put to use at last'. He enters burdened with his metaphysician's tools—half a dozen heavy books which he states in all seriousness are 'weighted with authority.' Because he is so serious about his function, subtle touches of comedy characterize Miller's initial presentation of Reverend Hale. But it is a humour which few audiences appreciate, so rapidly has the atmosphere of dread been spreading in the opening encounters of the drama. His mannered geniality and controlled friendliness, suggestive of the professional physician, lead him to express his conviction of the need for 'hard study if it comes to tracking down the Old Boy'. This doctor is unlikely to be an impartial diagnostician. Unexamined assumptions behind his learning are leading him to ludicrous attitudes and prejudiced deductions. These may be clearly seen by contrasting Hale's responses with the responses of Rebecca Nurse to the same situation.

REBECCA NURSE'S COMMON SENSE

Before his arrival the old, uneducated woman Rebecca had looked at the sick child. When Rebecca stood over her, the child had stopped whimpering. The old woman commented: 'A child's spirit is like a child, you can never catch it by run-ning after it; you must stand still, and, for love, it will soon it-self come back'. Her common sense then deflates the Put-nams' exaggerated anxieties and contrasts with the growing irrational fear in the household.

MRS. PUTNAM: My Ruth is bewildered, Rebecca; she cannot eat.

REBECCA: Perhaps she is not hungered yet.

Very different is Hale's response when informed of Ruth Put-nam's malady. A seriousness, so large that its implications to an audience are comic, characterizes his educated wonderment:

PUTNAM: We look to you to come to our house and save our child.

HALE: Your child ails too?

MRS. PUTNAM: Her soul, her soul seems flown away. She sleeps and yet she walks . . .

PUTNAM: She cannot eat.

HALE: Cannot eat! (*Thinks on it.*)

The common sense to say 'Perhaps she is not hungered yet' is buried beneath an edifice of learning which already tends towards searching out, and destroying, 'loose spirits.' His appearance of thoughtful impartiality has the effect of reinforcing a theological dogmatism; convinced that his books contain absolute truths, he asserts, 'with a tasty love of intellectual pursuit':

> Here is all the invisible world, caught, defined, and calculated. In these books the Devil stands stripped of all his brute disguises. Here are all your familiar spirits—your incubi and succubi; your witches that go by land, by air, and by sea; your wizards of the night and of the day. Have no fear now—we shall find him out if he has come among us, and I mean to crush him utterly if he has shown his face! (*He starts for the bed.*)

The ponderous phrases, the complex sentence structure, the mediaeval-like categorizing of spirits by their mode of travel and the times of their manifestations—all add to the ludicrousness of the learned gentleman. But it is a ludicrousness which can be dangerous for his terrible intensity is serving, ironically, to increase fears—as is shown by the interrogation he now conducts.

His mental attitude determines his method of questioning people in order to learn the causes of the children's illnesses. The questions are always based on the assumption that the devil exists and has been exerting his 'precise' influence in the community, rather as the interrogation of Arthur Miller always assumed that any association with the communist party was malignant and destructive to the American people. Whatever answers are given the interrogator, they merely consolidate his fundamental prejudice, so that a seemingly innocent occurrence becomes evidence of diabolical activity.

This mental attitude and this method of questioning, which in the structure of the play anticipate the attitudes and methods pervading the courtroom in Act Three, add to the developing tension and hysteria. Hale is the demanding interrogator: the people in the Reverend Parris's household are on the defensive. Abigail is under immediate pressure and forced to assert that she has never sold herself to the devil: 'I'm a good girl! I'm a proper girl!'

The appearance of Tituba makes Abigail implicate the black woman; the drinking of chicken's blood is interpreted by Hale as a means by which the West Indian woman has used the children for the devil's purposes. She has 'sent out' the devil's spirit and it has infected the young people. Abigail adds to the mounting evidence: 'She sends her spirit on me in church; she makes me laugh at prayer. . . She comes to me every night to go and drink blood. . . She comes to me while I sleep; she's always making me dream corruptions!' The rhythmic similarity of the sentences and repetitions of accusations are creating a *crescendo* effect as the scene moves to its climactic close.

Predictably, Hale accepts all these assertions; he has found one woman who has made a compact with the devil. The pressure of questioning moves to her and, frightened by the possibility of death and by the self-righteous intensity of the white masters surrounding her, Tituba suggests that 'somebody else be witchin' these children'.

At this, a name is required and the atmosphere of interrogation changes to one of enforced confession. The black woman, tormented by her own terror, names Sarah Good and Goody Osburn; at this moment Abigail rises, adds another name and Betty, affected by the voices of the others, breaks her silence and utters further names. The act concludes as though it were the hysterical climax to a religious service—but a service very different from, and contrasting with, Reverend Parris's earlier recitation of a psalm. Names are called as though in a litany; but the effect of this calling is that reputations are destroyed and people are being put under threat of torture and execution. Interrogation has led to forced confessions, confessions to an atmosphere of perverted religious participation. The atmosphere of dread has become an active, fear-filled hysteria. Much of the hysteria is still confined to the small upper bedroom of Parris's house, but it is to spread to other homes and bring terror to many innocent parishioners.

The Theme of Power in *The Crucible*

Christopher Bigsby

Christopher Bigsby writes that *The Crucible* is above all a study in power. According to Bigsby, power is in the hands of two major forces: the church, which has the power to define social and moral conditions, and the children, who suddenly find that they have gained access to power. Bigsby suggests that power in the play is seductive, infused with sexual overtones. The judges, for example, take a perverse, almost erotic pleasure in using the trial to provoke confessions that are defined by sexual forthrightness.

Bigsby also argues that power is in the hands of those who define the nature of reality for the towns-people. In *The Crucible*, church authorities have the power to establish and authorize the rules by which others must live. By recognizing only that of which he has immediate knowledge, John Proctor becomes a threat to the church. Bigsby argues that Proctor's challenge is to overcome the guilt that renders him power-less and transform it into conscience and responsibility, thereby acquiring the power to save himself.

Christopher Bigsby is a professor at the University of East Anglia, Norwich, England, where he is a senior lecturer in American literature. His major works include *Confrontation and Commitment: A Study of Contemporary American Drama, 1959–66, A Critical Introduction to Twentieth-Century American Drama, David Mamet,* and *Miller on File.*

Beyond anything else *The Crucible* is a study in power and the mechanisms by which power is sustained, challenged, and lost. Perhaps that is one reason why, as Miller has noted, productions of the play seem to precede and follow revolutions and why what can be seen as a revolt of the young against the old was, on the production of *The Crucible* in Communist China, perceived as a comment on the Cultural Revolution of the 1960s, in which the Young Guard humiliated, tortured, and even killed those who had previously been in authority over them: parents, teachers, members of the cultural elite. In the landscape of *The Crucible*, on the one hand stands the church, which provides the defining language within which all social, political, and moral debate is conducted. On the other stand those usually deprived of power—the black slave Tituba and the young children—who suddenly gain access to an authority as absolute as that which had previously subordinated them. Those ignored by history become its motor force. Those socially marginalized move to the very center of social action. Those whose opinions and perceptions carried neither personal nor political weight suddenly acquire an authority so absolute that they come to feel they can challenge even the representatives of the state. As Miller observes, in a note to the unpublished filmscript, Tituba "has the feel of a power she has never known in her life." To be a young girl in Salem was to have no role but obedience, no function but unquestioning faith, no freedom except a willingness to submit to those with power over her life. Sexuality was proscribed, the imagination distrusted, emotions focused solely on the stirring of the spirit. Rebellion, when it came, was thus likely to take as its target first those with least access to power, then those for whom virtue alone was insufficient protection. Next would come those who were regarded as politically vulnerable and finally those who possessed real power. Predictably it was at this final stage that the conspiracy collapsed, just as Senator McCarthy was to thrive on those who possessed no real purchase on the political system and to lose his credibility when he chose to challenge the U.S. Army. The first three witches named were a slave, a laborer's wife who had become little more than a tramp, and a woman who had absented herself from church and reportedly lived in sin.

THE THEME OF POWER

The Crucible is a play about the seductive nature of power and that seductiveness is perhaps not unconnected with a confused sexuality. The judges were people who chose not to inquire into their own motives. They submitted to the irrational with a kind of perverse pleasure, a pleasure not entirely drained of sexual content. They dealt, after all, with exposure, with stripping souls bare, with provoking and hearing confessions of an erotic forthrightness that no other occasion or circumstances would permit. They saw young women cry out in a kind of orgasmic ecstasy. They witnessed men and women of position, intelligence, and property rendered into their power by the confessions of those who recalled abuses and assaults, revealed to them only in a religiously and therapeutically charged atmosphere. These were the "recovered memories" of Puritan New England, and the irrational nature of the accusations, their sexual frisson, the lack of any proof beyond "spectral evidence" (the dreams and visions of the accusers) were a part of their lubricious attraction. When Mary Warren accuses a woman, she says, "I never knew it before . . . and all at once I remembered everything she done to me!" In our own time we are not so remote from this phenomenon as to render it wholly strange. Men and women with no previous memory of assaults, which were apparently barbaric and even demonic, suddenly recall such abuse, more especially when assisted to do so by therapists, social workers, or religionists who offer themselves as experts in the spectral world of suppressed memories. Such abuse, recalled in later life, is impossible to verify, but the accusations alone have sufficed to destroy entire families. To deny reality to such abuse is itself seen as a dangerous perversion, just as to deny witchcraft was seen as diabolic in Puritan New England.

Did the young girls in Salem, then, see no witches? Were they motivated solely by self-concern or, in Abigail's case, a blend of vengeance and desire? *The Crucible* is not concerned to arbitrate. Tituba plainly does dabble in the black arts, while Mrs. Putnam is quite prepared to do so. Abigail seems a more straightforward case. Jealous of Elizabeth Proctor, she sees a way of removing her and marrying John. In Miller's screenplay, however, Abigail has a vision of Elizabeth's spirit visiting her in her bedroom:

INT NIGHT ABIGAIL BEDROOM

She is asleep in bed. She stirs, then suddenly sits up and sees, seated in a nearby chair, a WOMAN with her back to her. ABIGAIL slides out of bed and approaches the woman, comes around to see her face—it is ELIZABETH PROCTOR.

ABIGAIL: Elizabeth? I am with God! In Jesus' name begone back to Hell!

ELIZABETH'S FACE is transformed into that of a HAWK, its beak opening. ABIGAIL steps back in terror.

POWER AND THE NATURE OF REALITY

Whatever her motives, she plainly sees this phantom even though it is conjured not from the devil but from guilt and desire, which in Puritan New England were seen as synonymous. In the screen version Abigail is described as "Certain now that she's mad." This takes us beyond the portrait we are offered by the play, where she is presented as more clearly calculating, but the essential point is not the nature of her motivation nor even the substantiality or otherwise of witches, but the nature of the real and the manner in which it is determined. Proctor and the others find themselves in court because they deny a reality to which others subscribe and in which, whatever their motives, they in part believe, until, slowly, skepticism begins to infect them with the virus of another reality.

It is the essence of power that it accrues to those with the ability to determine the nature of the real. They authorize the language, the grammar, the vocabulary within which others must live their lives. Miller observed in his notebook, "Very important. To say 'There be no witches' is to invite charge of trying to conceal the conspiracy and to discredit the highest authorities who alone can save the community!" Proctor and his wife try to step outside the authorized text. They will acknowledge only those things of which they have immediate knowledge. "I have wondered if there be witches in the world," observes John Proctor, incautiously, adding, "I have no knowledge of it," as his wife, too, insists: "I cannot believe it." When Proctor asserts his right to freedom of thought and speech—"I may speak my heart, I think"—he is reminded that this had been the sin of the Quakers, and Quakers of course had learned the limits of free speech and faith at the end of a hangman's noose on Boston Common.

PROCTOR'S TRANSFORMATION OF GUILT INTO POWER

There is a court that John and Elizabeth Proctor fear. It is one, moreover, which if it has no power to sentence them to death does nonetheless command their lives. Proctor says to his wife, "I come into a court when I come into this house!" Elizabeth, significantly, replies, "The magistrate sits in your heart that judges you." Court and magistrate are simply synonyms for guilt. The challenge for John Proctor is to transform guilt into conscience and responsibility. Guilt renders him powerless, as it had Willy Loman in *Death of a Salesman;* individual conscience restores personal integrity and identity, and places him at the center of social action. Miller has remarked of Proctor, "I suppose I had been searching a long time for a tragic hero, and now I had him; the Salem story was not going to be abandoned. The longer I worked the more certain I felt that improbable as it might seem, there were moments when an individual conscience was all that could keep the world from falling apart."

Despite the suspicions of his judges, though, Proctor does not offer himself as social rebel. If he seeks to overthrow the court, it is apparently for one reason only: to save his wife. But behind that there is another motive: to save not himself but his sense of himself. In common with so many other Miller protagonists, he is forced to ask the meaning of his own life. As Tom Wilkinson, who played the part of Proctor in a National Theatre production, has said, "It is rare for people to be asked the question which puts them squarely in front of themselves." But that is the question asked of John Proctor and that, incidentally, was asked of Miller in writing the play and later in appearing before HUAC.[1]

Miller seems to have written the play in a kind of white heat. The enthusiasm and speed with which he went to Salem underline the urgency with which he regarded the project, as did his later comment, on returning from Salem, that he felt a kind of social responsibility to see it through to production. His achievement was to control and contain that anger without denying it. Linguistically he achieved that by writing the play first in verse. Dramatically he accomplished it by using the structured formality of the court hearings, albeit hearings penetrated by the partly hysterical, partly calculated interventions of the accusing girls.

1. House Un-American Activities Committee

The Theme of Guilt in *The Crucible*

E. Miller Budick

E. Miller Budick writes that *The Crucible* is an exploration of guilt. Because of his adultery, John Proctor, who represents the human inclination to perceive oneself as sinful, defines himself as a fallen man. To Budick, the need to exonerate oneself from the evil of sinfulness forms the central theme of the play. Budick argues that the Proctors and the citizens of Salem look to justice to alleviate their feelings of sinfulness; but it is a harsh justice fed by anger and punishment. For Miller, charity is the missing element that would allow them to cope with their nagging sense of guilt.

E. Miller Budick teaches American studies and English at the Hebrew University of Jerusalem. He has written numerous articles and critiques on American literature.

Miller's play, we would all agree, is an argument in favour of moral flexibility. The fundamental flaw in the natures of the Puritan elders and by extension of the McCarthyites, as Miller sees it, is precisely their extreme tendency toward moral absolutism. "You must understand," says Danforth, "that a person is either with this court or he must be counted against it, there be no road between." But Miller is interested, not only in establishing the fact of such absolutism and condemning it, but also in isolating the factors which cause the rigidity which he finds so dangerous. And he is anxious to propose avenues of escape from the power of an over-active, absolutizing moral conscience. As we have seen, critics have objected to Miller's apparently one-sided moralizing in the play. But this moralizing, we must note, is concentrated almost exclusively in the prologue introductions to characters and scenes, and these narrative intrusions into the action of

Reprinted from "History and Other Specters in *The Crucible*," by E. Miller Budick, *Modern Drama*, vol. 28, no. 4 (December 1985), by permission of *Modern Drama*.

the play may no more represent Miller, the playwright, than Gulliver[1] represents Jonathan Swift[2] or Huck Finn, Mark Twain. Indeed, as other critics have pointed out, the play proper portrays a remarkably well-balanced community of saints and sinners which deserves our full attention and sympathy. Despite the annoying persistence of such unmitigated villainy as that represented by judges Danforth and Hathorne, there is moral education in the course of the drama (in Hale and Parris), while throughout the play such characters as Goody Nurse and Giles Corey represent unabated moral sanity and good will. Furthermore, John Proctor, the opponent of all that seems evil in the play, is not an uncomplicated hero. If we put aside for a moment Proctor's indiscretion with Abigail Williams, which itself has serious social, not to mention ethical, implications, Proctor, who has not taken his sons to be baptized, who does not appear regularly in church (all because of a personal dislike for the appointed representative of the church), and who does not respect Puritan authority even before the abhorrent abuse of power during the trials, does represent, if not an enemy, then at least a potential threat to a community which, Miller is quick to acknowledge, is involved in a life-death struggle to survive.

MORAL ARROGANCE OF THE MAIN CHARACTERS

In fact, it is in the ambiguous nature of the play's hero and his relationship to the rest of the community that Miller begins to confront the complexity of the work's major issue. For if the Salem judges suffer from an unabidable moral arrogance, so does John Proctor, and so, for that matter, do many other of the play's characters. *The Crucible* is a play seething with moral judgements on all sides, on the parts of its goodmen (and goodwomen) as well as of its leaders. The courts condemn the "witches," to be sure, and this act is the most flagrant example of over-zealous righteousness in the play. But the Proctors and their friends are also very free in their moral pronouncements (note the otherwise exemplary Rebecca's much resented "*note of moral superiority*" in Act One), as is Miller's own narrator, who, as we have already observed, is totally unselfconscious in his analyses of his Puritan forbears' ethical deficiencies. The point, I think, is that moral arrogance, the tendency to render unyielding judge-

1. protagonist of *Gulliver's Travels* 2. English satirist

ments, is not confined within the American power structure. It is at the very heart of the American temperament, and therefore it is at the heart of Miller's play as well. For *The Crucible* attempts to isolate the sources of moral arrogance, to determine the psychological and perceptual distortions which it represents, and thus to point the direction to correcting our moral optics.

Obviously John Proctor does not represent the same threat to freedom posed by Danforth and Hathorne. But this may be the point exactly, that Proctor does not possess the power, the authority, which converts stubborness, arrogance, guilt, and pride into social dangers. We must remember, however, that neither did the Puritans wield such dangerous authority until after they had ascended to power in the new world. The story of Proctor, therefore, may be in part the story of American Puritanism itself, Puritanism which wrestled with its own sense of original sin and damnation, which overcame enemies like the Anglican Church which would judge and persecute it, and which finally fought to establish the pure church, the church of the individual saints, in America. Proctor fails in his struggle against persecution of conscience. The Puritan church succeeded—but only for a time. Indeed, this apparent difference between Proctor and the Puritans serves only to stress how corrupting power can become in the hands of a certain kind of person, the Puritan American who is obsessed by his own guilt and driven by the desire to determine sanctity in himself and in others, and to make it conform to the visible human being.

THE FORCES OF GUILT AND SIN

As Miller himself states, guilt is a major force behind and throughout his drama. The major action of the play revolves, therefore, not around the courts and their oppression of the community (the natural analogue to the McCarthy trials), but rather around the figure of Miller's goodman, John Proctor. Miller's real interest resides neither in the sin of tyranny (the courts) nor in the crime of subversion (Proctor's rebellion from authority), but in the sources of tyranny and rebellion both, and in the metaphysical (or religious) assumptions and psychological pressures which cause individuals to persecute and be persecuted for arbitrarily defined crimes of conscience. The personal history of Proctor is the very best kind of history of the Puritan theocracy, just as the story of the

Puritans is the very best kind of history of America itself, for
both stories probe to the roots, not only of a community, but
of the very mentality which determined that community. It is
a most powerful irony of the play that Proctor is victimized
and destroyed by the very forces which, despite his apparent
opposition, he himself embodies. The witch trials do, as
Miller says in his "Echoes Down the Corridor," break "the
power of theocracy in Massachusetts." But the seeds of this destruction were less within the chimerical crime of witchcraft
than within the rigours of the Puritan definition of sainthood
which identified moral goodness with outward manifestations
of salvation, a belief which, as we shall see momentarily, characterized "witches" and judges alike. For, as the Puritans
themselves came to recognize, the implications of spectre evidence, the realization that the devil could assume the person
of a child of light, essentially undermined the Puritans' conviction in visible sanctity and hence in the possibility of a federal community predicated upon such sanctity. If devils could
parade as saints, how could one determine who in fact was
saved, who damned? The danger which Miller sees for his
contemporary American public is not that it will fail to recognize totalitarianism in the Puritans, or even in McCarthy.
Totalitarianism is too easy an enemy, as the McCarthy phenomenon itself demonstrates in its hysterical reaction to Communism. The danger is that the Americans will not be able to
acknowledge the extent to which tyranny is an almost inevitable consequence of moral pride and that moral pride is
part and parcel of an American way of seeing the world, an aspect of the tendency to externalize spiritual phenomena and
claim them as absolute and objective marks of personal or political grace.

The major historical fabrication of the play is, of course,
the adulterous relationship between Proctor and Abigail
Williams. Many explanations have been offered for this alter-
ation of the historical facts (Miller himself comments on it),
but the chief necessity for inventing this adultery is, I think,
that it provides precisely that inclination to perceive oneself
as sinful, as innately depraved, which characterizes both
Proctor and the Puritans, and which therefore delineates that
field of ambiguous moral constitution in which both the individual and his community must define and measure moral
"goodness." Proctor's adultery with Abigail establishes the
hero a fallen man, fallen even before the action of the play be-

gins. This may not be original sin as the Puritans defined it, but it is a sin which is prior and unrelated to the specific sin which the play explores, the covenanting of oneself to the devil, or, to put the problem in the more secular terminology that Miller would probably prefer, to the pursuing of a course of consummate, antisocial evil.

THE DESIRE FOR EXONERATION

The question being raised in Miller's play is this: on what basis can an individual exonerate himself of evil, knowing that he is indeed sinful and that according to his own beliefs he is damned? To put the question somewhat differently: how can John Proctor or any man believe in his own possible redemption, knowing what he does about the nature of his sexual, sinful soul? Our distance from Proctor's dilemma may enable us to understand levels of complexity which Proctor cannot begin to acknowledge. But this does not alter in the least the conflict which he must resolve. Nor does it protect us from analogous complexities in our own situations which we do not have the distance to recognize. Indeed, as Miller himself argues, "guilt" of the vague variety associated with Proctor was directly responsible for the "social compliance" which resulted in McCarthy's reign of terror in the 1950s: "Social compliance . . . is the result of the sense of guilt which individuals strive to conceal by complying. . . . It was a guilt, in this historic sense, resulting from their awareness that they were not as Rightist as people were supposed to be." Substituting "righteous" for Rightist, one has a comment equally valid for the Puritans.

Puritan theology, to be sure, had its own sophisticated answers to the question of the sinner's redemption. According to the Puritan church, the crucifixion of Christ represented the final act of reconciliation between man and God after man's disobedience in the garden of Eden had rent their relationship asunder. God in His infinite mercy chose to bestow upon certain individuals his covenant of grace, and thus to bring them, sinful as they might be, back into the congregation of the elect. God's will, in the process of election, was total, free, and inscrutable. Human beings were passive recipients of a gift substantially better than anything they deserved. This theological position is hinted at in the play when Hale pleads with Elizabeth Proctor to extract a confession from her husband:

> It is a mistaken law that leads you to sacrifice. Life, woman,
> life is God's most precious gift; no principle, however glorious,
> may justify the taking of it. . . . Quail not before God's judg-
> ment in this, for it may well be God damns a liar less than he
> that throws his life away for pride.

Miller has secularized and diluted Puritan theology in Hale's
speech, but the references to "sacrifice," "judgment," and
"pride" suggest the outlines of Christian history from the Puritan perspective, and they point to the central fact that divine
charity has made human sacrifice unnecessary, even pre-
sumptuous, in the light of the divine sacrifice which has already redeemed humankind.

But, as we shall see in a moment, factors other than the
covenant of grace had entered into the Puritans' religious
views, forcing a conflict already evident in the first generation of New Englanders, and threatening to tear the community apart by 1660, between a strict Calvinism on the one
hand and a federal theology on the other. This conflict was
essentially a competition between the covenant of grace,
which emphasized the charity implicit in Christ's crucifixion,
and the covenants of church and state, which were essential
to the Puritans' political objectives and which manifested
themselves as legal contracts designed to forge an identity
between inner grace and outer saintliness. In other words, in
demanding outward obedience to the federal form of government which they had conceived for their "city upon a hill,"
the organizers of the new community of saints had hedged
on their Calvinism; they had muted the doctrine of the ab-
soluteness of the covenant of grace, the ineffectiveness of
signs to evidence justification, in order to assert the importance of social conformity, of "preparation," and of an exter-
nal obedience to the covenant, not of grace, but of church and
state.

From one point of view, the tragedy of John Proctor, which
culminates in his execution for witchcraft, can be seen as
stemming from his and his wife's inability to relent in their
own moral verdicts, both of themselves and of each other,
and to forgive themselves for being human. It originates, in
other words, in their failure to understand the concept of divine charity which has effected their salvation and saved
them from damnation. "I am a covenanted Christian woman,"
Elizabeth says of herself, but neither she nor John seems to
understand what this covenant of grace means. Like the Pu-

ritan community of which they are a part, they seem to feel compelled personally to exact from themselves justice and to punish themselves for the sinfulness for which Christ's crucifixion has already atoned.

THE NEED FOR CHARITY

Not understanding the model of divine charity which determines their sanctity, they and their fellow Puritans are incapable of understanding the concept of charity at all. True, they plead charity. "We must all love each other now," exclaims Mary Warren in Act Two. "Excellency," pleads Hale, "if you postpone a week and publish to the town that you are striving for their confessions, that speak mercy on your part, not faltering." "You cannot break charity with your minister," Rebecca cautions John; "Learn charity, woman," Proctor begs Elizabeth; "Charity, Proctor, charity" asks Hale; "I have broke charity with the woman, I have broke charity with her," says Giles Corey. But even as they beg for mercy and sympathy, charity in the largest, most theologically meaningful sense of the word, they act in accordance, not with charity, but with that other component of the divine will—justice—which God has specifically chosen not to express by substituting the covenant of grace for His justifiable wrath. Thus, in the name of justice, Parris forces a confession from Abigail, Hale from Tituba; Abigail threatens Betty and the other girls; Proctor (significantly) does not *ask* Mary Warren to tell the truth but demands it of her, and so on. We know we are in terrible trouble when Hale, upon hearing of Rebecca's arrest, pleads with her husband to "rest upon the justice of the court." Justice alone simply will not do. Indeed, when justice forgets charity, it subverts the whole divine scheme of salvation, as the Puritans' theology had itself defined it.

Miller uses the issues of charity and justice both in order to locate the historical controversy which destroyed Salem, Massachusetts, and to develop an argument concerning the relationship between charity and justice as theological concepts, and charity and justice as the major features of human relationships—public and private. These issues, therefore, not only frame the play, but specifically define the relationship between John and Elizabeth Proctor, and they largely determine the course of their tragedy. In John and Elizabeth's first extended conversation, set in the "court" which is the Proctors' home, a play in miniature is enacted, a dramatic confrontation which explores the same issues of charity and justice portrayed in the play as a whole:

PROCTOR Woman . . . I'll not have your suspicion any more.

ELIZABETH . . . *I* have no—

PROCTOR I'll not have it!

ELIZABETH Then let you not earn it.

PROCTOR *with a violent undertone* You doubt me yet?

ELIZABETH *with a smile, to keep her dignity* John, if it were not Abigail that you must go to hurt, would you falter now? I think not. . . .

PROCTOR *with solemn warning* You will not judge me more, Elizabeth. I have good reason to think before I charge fraud on Abigail, and I will think on it. Let you look to your own improvement before you go to judge your husband any more. . . . Spare me! You forget nothin' and forgive nothin'. Learn charity, woman. I have gone tiptoe in this house all seven month since she is gone. I have not moved from there to there without I think to please you, and still an everlasting funeral marches round your heart. I cannot speak but I am doubted, every moment judged for lies, as though I come into a court when I come into this house! . . . I'll plead my honesty no more. . . . No more! I should have roared you down when first you told me your suspicion. But I wilted, and, like a Christian, I confessed. Confessed! Some dream I had must have mistaken you for God that day. But you're not, you're not, and let you remember it! Let you look sometimes for the goodness in me, and judge me not.

ELIZABETH I do not judge you. The magistrate sits in your heart that judges you. I never thought you but a good man, John— *with a smile*—only somewhat bewildered.

PROCTOR *laughing bitterly* Oh, Elizabeth, your justice would freeze beer! *He turns suddenly toward a sound outside. He starts for the door as Mary Warren enters. As soon as he sees her, he goes directly to her and grabs her by her cloak, furious.* How do you go to Salem when I forbid it? do you mock me? *Shaking her.* I'll whip you if you dare leave this house again!

What is important in this scene is not just that Elizabeth's lack of charity toward John leads directly to Proctor's lack of charity both toward Elizabeth and toward Mary Warren as she enters the house; or that this cycle of anger and recrimination causes further hostility on the parts of the two women who hold each other's and John's fate in their hands. (An analogous kind of reading could be made for John's confrontation with Abigail earlier in the play, when John not only fails to respond to Abigail's very real and understandable hurt ["Pity me, pity me!", she pleads], but absolutely refuses even to acknowledge that the affair ever occurred: "PROCTOR Wipe it out of mind. We never touched, Abby. ABIGAIL Aye, but we did. PROCTOR Aye, but we did not.") The point is not simply that anger begets anger, nor that the characters do not trust each other. Rather, the problem is that the characters have not admitted humankind's very paltry powers of moral judgement. They have not accepted in their hearts that God alone can render judgement on humankind. The characters of the play—*all* the characters, and not just Danforth and Hathorne—have mistaken themselves for God, to paraphrase Proctor, and this misunderstanding is precisely the problem. Elizabeth cannot see the "goodness" in John just as she cannot see the "goodness" in herself (and John, later, cannot see the "goodness" in himself), because what both John and Elizabeth have forgotten is that, according to their own beliefs, the goodness within them is not a natural goodness but the goodness implanted there by God's grace, despite the fact that they are, to apply Elizabeth's own words about herself, "so plain" and "so poorly made." We can expand the argument by pointing out John and Elizabeth's unwillingness to recognize that goodness is not contingent upon a single action or even upon a series of actions. Goodness does not depend upon what the Puritans would call "works." Rather, goodness is an indwelling potentiality— whether innate, for the secularists, or implanted there by God—which must be nurtured and allowed to express itself. On a larger theological scale, the fundamental problem for both John and Elizabeth is a lack of faith in true sense, a failure to recall their religion telling them that God has saved them *despite* the fact that they are sinners, and that the means of their salvation was divine charity itself.

Autobiographical Elements in *The Crucible*

John Elsom

John Elsom concludes that, to a large extent, Arthur Miller's behavior in front of the House Un-American Activities Committee (HUAC) mirrored John Proctor's confrontation with the authorities at Salem. When Miller received his subpoena in May 1956 he had to stand alone, like Proctor, as an individual facing malign social pressures. According to Elsom, Miller maintained his dignity, and, like John Proctor, held to his moral convictions and refused steadfastly to give names.

Elsom argues that Proctor is a tragic hero in the Aristotelian sense. His flaw, his lust for Abigail, brings him down, but ultimately a higher justice prevails and Proctor gains an awareness of his own identity. Proctor learns, as Aristotle says a hero must, that an individual is morally responsible for his own life. In *The Crucible* and other of his plays, Miller explores the relationship of the individual to society and the societal pressures that act on him. In the modern world, these pressures move beyond the small community and, hence, are increasingly more difficult to understand.

John Elsom has worked as a college instructor, script reader for Paramount Pictures, and theater critic for *Listener.* His writings include *Theatre Outside London, Post-War British Theatre,* and *The History of the National Theatre.*

In May 1956, Arthur Miller received a HUAC subpoena in Reno, Nevada, outside the offices of a divorce lawyer, Mr Hills, who was smoothing the transition between his first wife and his second, Marilyn Monroe. He did not try to evade the summons: on the contrary. Hills, a pillar of the establishment judging by the citations on his walls, warned him that it was coming and showed him an escape by the back door, while a fellow client, Carl Royce, a rich cowboy who reminded Miller of John Wayne, offered him a haven on his ranch and a private plane to get there.

Miller described these gestures of support as 'a thoroughly American anarchism' for which he had 'developed a lot of respect as our last stand against fascist decorum'. But he chose to leave by the front door and when he met the HUAC investigator by the lift, he enquired, 'Are you looking for me?' In such ways did Miller acknowledge the state's right to call its citizens to account, while reserving his right as a citizen to say 'No'.

He appeared before HUAC a year later and steadfastly refused to name names. He even went on the attack. He produced an expert witness to assert that his plays were not communist and that he himself was not under communist discipline. This was unprecedented. In previous cases, expert witnesses had only appeared for the prosecution. Eventually, the Committee fined him $500 for contempt of Congress and sentenced him to a month in jail, suspended; and in 1958, the Supreme Court reversed this decision. 'Historically', Miller wrote, 'we were in the narrow trough between the grandiose anti-Communist crusade and the next ennobling cause, the war in Vietnam'.

Miller was indignant that he had been convicted at all, but his light sentence almost amounted to an apology. His dignified manner at his hearing may have helped. It drew the press to his side. The *New Republic*, which described him as 'the passionately self-exploring, artist-genius type', praised him for staying 'cool and unemotional' under fire. He was 'impressive'. His stance evoked Hollywood memories from the old days where a young Henry Fonda battled for plain folk against corruption.

Miller had prepared his mind to cope with his ordeal and this was not surprising, for the plays on which his reputation was already securely based, and the genre to which they belong, were much concerned with how an individual stood up against malign social pressures, or failed to do so. He adapted Ibsen's *An Enemy of the People* (1950) for Broadway; and it could be argued that McCarthyism was like the poison

WHY MILLER IS CALLED BEFORE HUAC

In a 1966 issue of Paris Review, Arthur Miller was asked by interviewers Olga Carlisle and Rose Styron to comment on his appearance before the House Un-American Activities Committee. Miller suggests that his refusal to allow the committee chairman to be photographed with his actress wife, Marilyn Monroe, initiated his trouble with HUAC.

INTERVIEWER: Was it the play, *The Crucible* itself, do you think, or was it perhaps that piece you did in the *Nation*—"A Modest Proposal"—that focused the Un-American Activities Committee on you?

MILLER: Well, I had made a lot of statements and I had signed a great many petitions. I'd been involved in organizations, you know, putting my name down for 15 years before that. But I don't think they ever would have bothered me if I hadn't married Marilyn. Had they been interested they would have called me earlier. And in fact I was told on good authority that the then Chairman, Francis Walter, said that if Marilyn would take a photograph with him, shaking his hand, he would call off the whole thing. It's as simple as that. Marilyn would get them on the front pages right away. They had been on the front pages for years, but the issue was starting to lose its punch. They ended up in the back of the paper or on the inside pages, and here they would get right up front again. These men would time hearings to meet a certain day's newspaper. In other words, if they figured the astronauts were going up, let's say, they wouldn't have a hearing that week; they'd wait until they'd returned and things had quieted down.

Matthew C. Roudané, ed., *Conversations with Arthur Miller.* Jackson: University Press of Mississippi, 1987.

in the system against which Dr. Stockmann ardently campaigned. A closer parallel, however, was with *The Crucible;* and in *Timebends,* Miller compared his expert witness, Harry Cain, with the Reverend Hale, who tried to undo the damage caused by his previous false witness.

JOHN PROCTOR AS A TRAGIC HERO

The likeness which struck almost everyone else was between Miller himself and John Proctor, the play's hero, because he refused to bear witness against others and in his manner of doing so, his moral stand. Technically, the character of Proctor was developed along the lines recommended for tragic heroes in A.C. Bradley's *Shakespearian*

Tragedy (1904), one reason why *The Crucible* was considered to be more of a tragedy than Miller's other plays which also ended in calamity: *All My Sons* (1947), *Death of a Salesman* (1949) and *A View from the Bridge* (1956). Bradley's book was a standard text in English-speaking universities and influenced many dramatists of the period, including T.S. Eliot and Eugene O'Neill. Bradley's theories were based upon Aristotle's *The Poetics* (c. 335 BC), the point of departure for most Western literary criticism, which he simplified and brought up to date to fit not only Shakespeare but other demands of the modern world.

Bradley followed Aristotle by asserting that the tragic hero should be a man (or woman) 'above average', but with a character flaw which circumstances exploit, thus bringing about his/her downfall. At the crisis, when the information about the main story has been gathered in and the outcome is in sight, a new enlightenment dawns—that, beyond the suffering, higher justice prevails. Tragic heroes rarely went quietly. Either from what they say about themselves or from what others say about them, their fates are turned into parables for mankind, a task which, according to many critics, was better tackled in verse than prose.

The flaw in Proctor's character was that he had lusted after the servant-girl, Abigail, whose jealousy brought to the surface the madness in Salem. The crisis came when Proctor chose to face death rather than lend support to the witch-hunters:

> HALE: Man, you will hang! You cannot!
>
> PROCTOR (his eyes full of tears): I can. And there's your first marvel, that I can. You have made your magic now, for now I see some shred of goodness in John Proctor. Not enough to weave a banner with, but white enough to keep it from such dogs.

This may not count as poetry, but within Miller's dour restraint elsewhere in the play, it ranked as heightened prose; and the moral point was succinctly made. By standing firm, Proctor lost his life, but regained the self-respect that his affair with Abigail had nearly cost him. The crucible burnt but purified.

PARALLELS BETWEEN JOHN PROCTOR AND MILLER

Something similar (without the hanging) may have happened to Miller at the HUAC hearing. As *Timebends* reveals, he was feeling guilty about his divorce. His marriage to

Monroe had turned him from being a retiring writer into the kind of star (tarnished by scandal) which HUAC in its dying days needed to persecute. He could have escaped, but he did not want to subject Monroe to unwelcome publicity. He thus shouldered his burden like a man and turned defeat into a moral victory.

Miller himself was nearly a tragic hero, as defined by Bradley, but Bradley's views on this matter were not quite the same as Aristotle's. One bone of contention lay in what was meant by 'above average'. Aristotle expected that the hero should come from a noble family, a guardian of the *polis* or city state; but even for an Edwardian critic like Bradley, this sounded snobbish. Bradley extended the definition to those who were above average in ability, education and moral insight. That was one reason why Joe Keller in *All My Sons* and Willy Loman in *Death of a Salesman* were not rated as tragic heroes. Of *Death of a Salesman*, [drama critic] Eric Bentley remarked that 'the theme arouses pity but no terror. Man is here too little and too passive to play the tragic hero'. Proctor came closer to the heroic stature, as did Miller.

Bradley established a connection between the hero's flaw and his downfall, which thus became a punishment. Aristotle was less specific. The gods must have some reason to torment him, for otherwise they would be unjust; but the hero could be the victim of someone else's flaws or of a revenge cycle which stretched back for generations. He could be under instructions from rival gods. Humility might pacify the gods, as pride would antagonise them, but Aristotle left room for the idea that the fates might simply conspire against the hero, without assistance on his part.

Bradley pointed out, however, that at some level, all of Shakespeare's heroes had caused their fates. If Lear had been less arrogant, Hamlet less indecisive, Macbeth less credulous and Othello less prone to jealousy, their downfalls could have been avoided. They had nobody to blame but themselves, however harsh this judgement may seem. The disaster was not their fault, but they had contributed to it. Bradley nudged tragic theory towards the notion that individuals were morally responsible for their lives, which, as [American diplomat] George Kennan might have pointed out, was the underlying assumption of all liberal democracies. Without it, the institutions of the Free World would collapse, trial by jury, the free press and elections. It was a principle which the West had to accept if its system of government was to survive at all.

In the 1950s, however, science and communism had in their different ways laid the burden on liberals to prove to what extent individuals could be considered to be 'free', bearing in mind that their lives were conditioned by so many factors outside their control, including language. If human beings were not free, they could not be held responsible, morally or otherwise. In an essay, 'On social plays', Miller argued that it was easier for a citizen in ancient Greece to believe that he was responsible for what happened in his society, because 'the *polis* were small units, apparently deriving from an earlier tribal organization, whose members probably knew one another personally. . . . The preoccupation of Greek drama with ultimate law, with the Grand Design, so to speak, was therefore an expression of a basic assumption of the people, who could not conceive, luckily, that any man could long prosper unless his *polis* prospered'.

But the United States was too big for such a connection easily to be made, not only geographically but in the diversity and range of its ethnic groups. Beneath the formal shell of its eighteenth-century Constitution, what was left of America but a seething mass of sectional interests? This was why on one level, the idea of federal nationhood had to be sustained by flag-waving patriotism and the American Dream, while on another, the daunting size of the US drove its inhabitants into self-protecting tribal packs, smaller even than the Greek *polis*, the nuclear family, an enclave of Italian immigrants, a farm in the prairies, a huddle of settlers' shacks by the Rockies.

Show-business contributed to national stability by providing the United States with images of its scale and its compensating homeliness. The lone cowboy riding the range was one sign for the continental vastness, while another might be the whistle-stop odysseys of a Hollywood bio-pic. But America's most popular play was, and still is, Thornton Wilder's *Our Town* (1938). Grover's Corners, New Hampshire, became the Hollywood model for small-town life, where stars like Monroe played the girls-next-door.

THE CRUCIBLE AS SOCIAL DRAMA

Miller wanted to show the shadows behind the radiant screen, how neighbourliness concealed moral evasions and how the American Dream of self-made success bore down heavily on middle-aged has-beens and never-weres, like Willy Loman. In his youth during the 1920s and 1930s, he had watched his father, a manufacturer, succumb to the Depression. He blamed the capitalist system and toyed with communism; but after the war, Stalinism so damaged his faith that he lost interest in party politics altogether. But he did not become disillusioned with the older definition of politics, that is, how the individual relates to the *polis*. That was his main concern for ten years until, after *A View from the Bridge* (1956), he seemed to suffer from a prolonged writer's block, which has been blamed upon his relationship with Monroe.

He wrote a film script for her, *The Misfits* (1960), but no new stage play until *After the Fall* (1964). This was taken to be an account of their marriage, but written in an odd style, with flashbacks and dream sequences, loosely connected by narration. It was as if Miller had lost confidence not only in politics and his marriage, but in his former way of looking at the world. The question marks which hovered over his social dramas and prevented some critics from calling them tragedies, had not faded with the years, but grown ever darker. His plays may have offered a strong retort to the optimism of [American playwright and director] George Abbott, they may have revealed the halo of darkness surrounding the American Dream, but they still lacked the inevitability of classical tragedy.

Would Loman, for example, have killed himself, if he had had a good year as a salesman and his son had made the football team? Probably not. Would Keller in *All My Sons* have been innocent, if his factory had supplied non-defective parts to warplanes which then went on to drop nuclear bombs on Japan? Possibly so, in which case the question arose as to the meaning of 'all'. Did it extend to all American servicemen, to all the Allied Forces—or to humanity at large? Keller and Loman did not have to contend with unseen forces or irreconcilable dilemmas, only with a society which placed a high premium on material success.

The humanisation of tragedy after Bradley led on to the idea that if societies behaved sensibly, all would be well. Soviet critics had already pronounced tragedy dead. In a modern world, controlled by scientific communism, it had no place. This seemed to be reassuring. Modern man did not need to fear the wrath of the gods. But it increased the scale of human responsibility immeasurably, beyond that of the *polis* to the world itself. There was no point where personal responsibility ended and destiny began. We were all Atlases, upholding the globe.

Classical tragedy explored the frontier between faith and reason. In ancient Greek, it was characterized by the distinction between *mythos* and *logos*, both of which simply meant a 'word' or a 'sign', but in different senses. *Logos* was used for a sign whose validity could be established by personal experience or reason; whereas *mythos* meant a sign whose validity rested upon divine revelation or unprovable assumptions. All languages were held to contain provable and unprovable elements, which made it easier to describe where reason had to give way to faith.

By the 1950s, that distinction had been long lost. Social drama assumed that there must always be a rational explanation somewhere, which was why *The Crucible* failed to generate the same degree of pity and terror as, for example, *Hamlet* or *The Bacchae* of Euripides. Miller and his audiences assumed that the devil did not exist and that what happened in Salem must have been caused by credulity, moral weakness and sexual hysteria. If this is not assumed, Proctor's dilemma becomes more alarming, for he would have to decide whether Abigail's frenzy was solely caused by jealousy or whether diabolic forces were not also at work. If he chose wrongly, all hell would break loose.

CHAPTER 3

Evaluating
The Crucible

READINGS ON
THE CRUCIBLE

The Dramatic Structure of *The Crucible*

Bernard F. Dukore

Bernard F. Dukore suggests that the dramatic structure of *The Crucible* is centered around an organizing
motif for each of the four acts. He identifies the central motif of act 1 as the attempt to place blame. In an
effort to save herself, Abigail blames others. Likewise,
Tituba, taking her cue from Abigail, absolves herself
by giving the authorities names. In act 2, the dominant motif is the court's threefold intrusion into the
Proctor home: first, when Mary Warren, Proctor's servant, returns from Salem as an official of the court;
second, when Hale arrives on court business; and
third, when Cheever appears at Proctor's door with
an official warrant to arrest Elizabeth. According to
Dukore, the dominant motif of act 3 is the assessment
of reliability of both the accused and the accusers.
The action moves to the public courtroom, where
Proctor challenges Abigail's credibility and Judge
Danforth tests the reliability of both Mary Warren
and Elizabeth. The organizing motif of act 4 is the
confession of guilt. Proctor's private sin of adultery
prompts him to confess to the public sin of consorting with the devil, ultimately resulting in his death.

Bernard Dukore is a professor of theater arts and
humanities at Virginia Polytechnic Institute in Blacks-
burg. He has written extensively about the theater,
playwrights, and dramatic theory and criticism.

Whereas the structure of *Death of a Salesman* is compact in
the Ibsenite or Hellenic manner, that of *The Crucible* is
panoramic in the Shakespearean manner, requiring relatively
little exposition at the start. The play divides into two parts,
each with two acts. Both involve integrity, which dominates

Excerpted from *"Death of a Salesman" and "The Crucible": Text and Performance*, by
Bernard F. Dukore (Atlantic Highlands, NJ: Humanities Press International, 1989).
Reprinted by permission of Macmillan Press Ltd.

the second part, wherein Proctor confesses to adultery, the private sin (Act III), and denies witchcraft, the public sin (Act IV). Despite the fusion of private and public spheres in both parts, the settings of the first are private residences (Parris's and Proctor's homes), of the second public arenas (trial room and jail cell). These locales mirror the thematic concerns, which moving outwards towards the public arena suggest a broadening of scope to embrace the Massachusetts colony.

Each act has a major motif and contrast between beginning and end. The chief motif of Act I is the attempt to find blame for both private and public problems; physical illness becomes a sign of moral illness, thus of the battle between God and the Devil. Whereas Act I begins with prayer, it ends with ecstatic cries about the Devil. The central motif of Act II is the court's gradual invasion of the Proctor home. Quasi-judicial hearings turn from the private to the public. The act begins with John Proctor returning home; it ends with his wife leaving. At the start, they are physically together yet emotionally separated; at the end, physically separated yet emotionally united, as he prepares to risk his reputation to save her life. Act III's dominant motif is the establishment of the credibility of accuser and accused. It opens with an off-stage voice charging a woman with witchcraft, which she denies; it closes with a man charged with working for the Devil, but instead of denying it he calls everyone in the room, including himself, guilty. Confession of guilt is the principal motif of the final act. In contrast with the first, the blame is of oneself rather than others. Whereas Elizabeth confesses herself guilty of her husband's adultery, he confesses to witchcraft but recants his confession. Act IV begins with people drinking spirits and joking about the Devil; it ends with a man affirming his virtue by going through death to God.

THE BLAME MOTIF OF ACT I

The first scenic unit of Act I primarily concerns Parris and Abigail. The doctor's report that Betty's illness may be attributable to unnatural causes involves an effort to avoid taking blame (for ignorance to a cure). When Parris is terrified that the doctor may be correct, Abigail decisively orders the messenger to remain silent. Like Parris, she wants to keep this public issue private. When he questions her about what happened in the woods, she gives excuses and false oaths. Admitting the girls danced, she denies they conjured spirits, calls Tituba's invocations Barbados songs and swears no one was naked. In the second scenic unit, superstition and rumour enter with the Putnams. When Ann reveals that her daughter Ruth joined the girls to conjure the dead to learn why Ann's children died in infancy, Abigail covers her lie with another: she herself did no conjuring, Tituba and Ruth did. Anticipating later developments, which include Hale's efforts to persuade the condemned to lie (immoral means) to save their lives (a righteous end), Ann tried to commune with infernal spirits (evil means) to beget children who will live (a righteous end).

Alone for the first time, the girls reveal the truth. Abigail's influence over them foreshadows her ability to influence the court. To ensure that everyone tells the same story, she explains what the others know and do not know. She brutally shakes Betty and threatens to beat her. Terrified, Betty darts from the bed, calling for her dead mother. The effect of conversations about witchcraft on a susceptible adolescent girl foreshadows what will occur in court. Though inert, Betty has subliminally absorbed the conversation. To fly to her mother, she tries to leave through the window, then reveals another lie of Abigail, who drank blood as a charm to kill Elizabeth.

When Proctor is alone with Abigail, we learn that they had committed adultery but that he, unlike she, determines not to resume their affair. Insisting she wipe their relationship from her mind, he declares that they never touched each other. As he will discover, repentance does not come so easily. Furthermore, his statement is a lie and, as the play reiterates, God damns liars.

As a crowd scene follows their intimate scene, personal sin (adultery) connects to public sin (witchcraft). Parishioners downstairs sing a psalm, Abigail attempts to entice Proctor sexually and Betty screams. Led by Parris, the singers rush into the room. Ann Putnam concludes that since Betty began to scream when she heard the psalm, it must be because she could not bear God's name.

Hale's entry signals another impulse in the dramatic action, another stage in the motif of blame. His questioning draws further admissions from Abigail, who to save herself blames others: there was soup and a frog jumped into it, she did not call the Devil but Tituba did, she and Betty drank none of the brew but Tituba tried to make her do so, she and

Betty drank blood but at Tituba's instigation, Tituba's spirit came to her at church to make her laugh at prayer, Tituba appeared while she slept and denuded her. Taking her cue from Abigail's denial of guilt and blame of others as witches, Tituba absolves herself by naming others. As though inspired and enraptured, Abigail begs to return to Jesus, confirms Tituba's names and adds another. With increasing theatrical momentum, the girls cite more names. On their ecstatic shrieks, the act ends.

THE INTRUSION OF THE COURT, ACT II

Structurally, the major thrust of the second act is the intrusion of the court into the Proctor home until the Proctors are separated. Initially, their major concern is private. John tries to placate Elizabeth but she merely '*receives*' his kiss. Their apartness is visualised: he stands by the doorway, his back to her, she by the basin, her back to him, the room between them. The invasion of the court into their home begins when she discloses that their servant Mary is now an official of the court, which has imprisoned fourteen people, whom it might hang. Their discussion of his infidelity employs legal terminology. He urges her to judge him no longer, as if their home were a courtroom, declares he will no longer plead his honesty, and recalls he had confessed his transgression to her. She asserts that a magistrate in his own heart judges him.

The public court further intrudes when Mary returns from Salem to disclose more arrests, a death sentence, and (foreshadowing) the court's view that inability to remember the ten commandments is proof of guilt. Although she gives Elizabeth a doll she made in court that day, she discloses that Elizabeth was mentioned—evidence to the prescient wife that Abigail wants her dead so she may replace her. Whereas the court has entered the Proctor home, Elizabeth wants her husband to enter the court to tell the truth about Abigail.

As a witch-hunter in a theocratic state, Hale arrives on court business, for which he uses an obvious euphemism: questions about the home's Christian character. When Proctor can recite only nine commandments, Elizabeth prompts the tenth, the injunction against adultery. Ineffectively, he tries to joke his forgetfulness away with the quip that between them they know all ten. When Elizabeth asks him to tell Hale the truth about the girls' accusations, he repeats what Abigail had told him on the day Hale arrived. Hale reluctantly admits to a misgiving that some confessed for fear of being hanged if they denied the charge.

As in Act I, a crowd scene climaxes Act II. Apart from the theatrical effectiveness of a large number of people following a small number, the crowd helps give Proctor stature, since it congregates at his home, as if he were a leader (for a person of low rank, this is like a king's court in seventeenth-century drama). This sequence more openly discusses the proceedings of the court, which private vengeance uses for its own ends. Cheever represents the court's official entry into the Proctor home, since he is a clerk who has come with a warrant to arrest Elizabeth, charged by Abigail with trying to kill her by sticking needles in a doll. After Elizabeth's arrest, Proctor forces Mary to join him in denouncing Abigail in court, despite the possibility that his adultery will be revealed. Private and public terms of trial merge and Mary's repeated declaration 'I cannot' anticipates important developments in the next act.

THE CREDIBILITY OF ACCUSER AND ACCUSED, ACT III

In Act III, the play moves into the courtroom, a public arena that deliberates public guilt but where private guilt will also emerge. Whereas the act concludes with a full courtroom, it starts with an empty room. For a full page, one hears off-stage voices. When a prisoner and a court official enter, the terror of the court invades the room visually as well as vocally. Early argument foreshadows the act's major motif, the establishment of the truthfulness of accuser and accused. While the girls assert that the upright Rebecca Nurse sent her spirit to murder seven babes, argues Proctor, one of them will swear she lied. The accused Elizabeth has claimed to be pregnant, which would spare her life, but though Judge Danforth is sceptical, Proctor insists she never lies.

Did Proctor threaten Mary to make her sign the deposition? To help determine whether Mary lied then or now, Danforth questions Abigail, who denies Mary's claim that she saw her make the doll in court and stick a needle into it for safekeeping. Proctor accuses her of trying to murder his wife, he cites her removal from church for laughter during prayers, and when he accuses her of having led the other girls to the woods at night to dance naked, Hale confirms that Parris had told him these facts when he arrived in Salem. If as Mary claims she pretended to turn cold and have

an icy skin, let her now demonstrate the truth of this assertion, the court demands. Repeating what she reiterated at
the end of Act II, Mary simply says she cannot. She is unable
to explain why.

To Danforth's query as to whether she might have been
mistaken about seeing spirits, Abigail responds with indignation, a warning of hell's powers, and an enactment of
what Mary had called pretence. Claiming a cold wind has
descended, she acts frightened. Through chattering teeth,
she asks why Mary, her accuser, has done this. Echoing her
words at the end of Act II, Mary hysterically cries that she
cannot.

To destroy Abigail's credibility, knowing that he will also
destroy himself, Proctor interrupts, calls her a whore and
confesses to adultery. To prove his truthfulness, also foreshadowing his concern at the end, he points out that a man
will not easily relinquish his good name. Elizabeth, he says,
dismissed Abigail from their employ because of adultery.

What follows has been variously called one of those
'tricky twists of plot that Sardou himself might have admired' (Julius Novick, *Village Voice*, 4 May 1972) and 'no
mere trick of melodrama' for it grows 'from a character'
(Philip Hope-Wallace, *Manchester Guardian*, 11 April 1956).
Elizabeth, who Proctor had insisted is incapable of lying—is
brought to confirm his accusation. In a theatrically vivid
moment, Danforth has Proctor and Abigail turn their backs
to each other and instructs them not to speak to Elizabeth,
whom he places between them. When Danforth asks why
she dismissed Abigail, Elizabeth to save her husband's name
hedges. Asked whether he is an adulterer, she lies for the
same reason—which confirms Abigail and condemns him.
Elizabeth thus enters her own purgatory, or crucible, from
which she emerges in the next act.

Irrefutably reestablishing the credibility of the initial accuser, the previous arguments are theatricalised. With a
bloodcurdling shriek, Abigail points to the ceiling and ad-
dresses a yellow bird. Apparently possessed, as in Act I, she
and the other girls try to persuade the bird not to attack them
for doing God's work. First Abigail, then all the girls repeat
Mary's statements. Verbal and nonverbal unite. Demanding
they stop pretending, Mary stamps her feet, then raises her
fists; they repeat demand, stamp and gesture. The girls rush
about, fearful of a swooping bird, until Mary, '*as though in-*

fected', screams with them. Gradually, Abigail and the others stop, until only Mary stares at the bird, madly screaming. She accuses Proctor of being the Devil's instrument, asserts that he wants her name and accuses him of trying to overthrow the court. When Danforth charges Proctor with joining the Antichrist, he denounces the court. Then Hale does—a different kind of echo from the previous one.

Three months precede the last act. The prison and cemetery population has increased, with the result that orphans wander the town, abandoned cattle bellow, crops rot and people fear that they may become victims of the court. Rebellion against the courts, which has broken out in nearby Andover, threatens Salem.

THE CONFESSION OF GUILT, ACT IV

The start of Act IV is a distorting mirror of the start of Act I. In Act I, a girl sleeps and a minister prays in vain to waken her; in Act IV, Sarah Good and Tituba sleep and a jailer succeeds in waking them. Instead of invoking God, as the minister does in Act I, the women invoke the Devil. Whereas the first act exposition reveals that the girls drank chicken blood, the fourth act has the women and their jailer drink cider and the Marshall enters almost drunk. Whereas characters in Act I deny traffic with the Devil, those in Act IV are anxious to join him, since Barbados and Hell are desirable places to fly to on so cold a day. Those who helped to establish guilt are revealed to be criminals; with Mercy, Abigail has run away after breaking into Parris's strongbox and stealing all his money.

Although Parris tries to persuade Danforth to postpone further executions until Hale has convinced someone to confess, Danforth refuses since to delay, reprieve or pardon might cast doubt on the guilt of those he has already had killed. His own reputation as an honest jurist, his name, has become more important than the basis of a good name. Ironically, evidence of Elizabeth's truthfulness arrives: she is well on in her pregnancy.

Since Proctor has not seen her for three months, Danforth and Parris think she might be instrumental in making him confess. Ironically, she confesses to him (provocation to commit adultery). Because his private sin initially prompts him to accept the same verdict for his public sin, he confesses to the latter. Recognising their differences, however, he renounces the confession to die with honour, goodness and name intact.

The foregoing analysis omits a scene Miller added six months after opening night. Inserted between the second and third acts, it has Proctor meet Abigail in the forest to warn her what he will do if she does not change her accusation of his wife. Abigail, who has come to believe her lies, cannot imagine he will confess. The chief advantage of the scene is psychological exploration of Abigail. Its disadvantages are interruption of the dramatic momentum from arrest to trial, overemphasis on the psychological and personal aspects of the play, diminution of the impact of Act III (with Abigail forewarned of what will happen) and weakening of credibility (would Proctor arrange a clandestine meeting with her on the eve of confessing their adultery?). Although the scene is not in *Collected Plays*, it appears as an Appendix to the Bantam paperback and in Weales's[1] edition of text and commentary.

1. critic Gerald

Strengths and Flaws in *The Crucible*

Ronald Hayman

Ronald Hayman finds much to admire in *The Crucible*. According to Hayman, Salem's superstition and acrimony make it ripe for an explosion of hysteria. Miller organizes the four acts of the play to show how negative forces converge to create the terror of the witch-hunt. Miller also offers the audience an insight into the psychological workings of a court that places its own credibility above justice. Hayman applauds Miller's flexible use of seventeenth-century dialect.

However, Hayman argues, in a rewrite of the play Miller broke the simplicity of the original and included some overdone and flowery passages. Hayman also dislikes Miller's shift of focus in the last act from the social emphasis to a spotlight on John Proctor.

Ronald Hayman is a contributor to the Frederick Ungar World Dramatists Series. His works include *Edward Albee, Arthur Miller,* and *John Osborne.*

Structurally *The Crucible* is as different from *Death of a Salesman* as *Death of a Salesman* is from *All My Sons.* Miller returns to a chronological narrative but takes a bigger cast of characters and moves between different locales. The hero, instead of being representative of his society, stands out against it, and dies because (unlike Willy Loman) he is not sufficiently separated from values that endure. Like Shaw's[1] St. Joan he is so eager to stay alive that he makes the "confession" that is required of him, only to tear it up afterward, knowing that if he puts his name to it he will never "find himself" again. Identity is more precious than survival.

1. Irish dramatist George Bernard

Excerpted from *World Dramatists: Arthur Miller,* by Ronald Hayman. Copyright © 1970, 1972 by Ronald Hayman. Reprinted with the permission of The Continuum Publishing Company.

SALEM'S ACRIMONIOUS ATMOSPHERE

Ranged against him is almost the whole of Salem society, which Miller rightly shows both before and during the witch hunt. In the first few minutes of action he establishes a strong and suspenseful situation. Rev. Parris's young daughter Betty is lying in a stupor and Rev. Hale, a specialist in diabolical possession, is on his way over. After this, the play can afford a passage of more leisurely dialogue to build up a quick picture of a Puritan community in which the acquisitive urge is as strong as the religious and in which the soil is ready for a witch hunt that thrusts down such powerful roots so frighteningly quickly.

As Arthur Miller has said:

> The central impulse for writing . . . was not the social but the interior psychological question, which was the question of that guilt residing in Salem which the hysteria merely unleashed, but did not create.

The play was written before he was himself a victim of McCarthyism, but he was already aware that what was driving the conformists to join in the witch hunt was a sense of their own guilt and a panicky desire to cover it up. The pattern in Salem was the same, as Miller indicates by the way he uses his large cast of supporting characters. Rev. Parris suffers from a persecution complex. Giles Corey is suspicious of his wife because she reads books. Ann Putnam, who has lost seven babies within a day of giving birth to them, is eager to think that unnatural causes are at work, and the predatory Thomas Putnam is always litigating against his neighbors. Superstition and acrimony are rife and the sermons are mostly about hell-fire.

SALEM'S FORCES OF TERRORIZATION

The spacing out of the four sequences that make up the play's four acts is determined largely by the necessity of showing how the forces of terrorization join together. After its quiet beginning, the first act ends hysterically with Tituba, the Negress slave, Abigail, the ringleader of the troublemakers, and Betty all denouncing other women in order to protect themselves. And before the act reaches this climax, it shows us in Rev. Hale's cross-examination of Abigail and Tituba how the outlines of truth can dissolve in the smoke screen of instant fiction that both of them throw out in self-defense.

HALE: You cannot evade me, Abigail—Did your cousin drink any of the brew in that kettle?

ABIGAIL: She never drank it!

HALE: Did you drink it?

ABIGAIL: No, sir!

HALE: Did Tituba ask you to drink it?

ABIGAIL: She tried but I refused.

HALE: *Why* are you concealing? Have you sold yourself to Lucifer?

ABIGAIL: I never sold myself! I'm a good girl—I—[*Ann enters with Tituba.*] I did drink of the kettle!—She made me do it! She made Betty do it!

TITUBA: Abby!

ABIGAIL: She makes me drink blood!

PARRIS: Blood! !

ANN: My baby's blood?

TITUBA: No—no, chicken blood, I give she chicken blood!

HALE: Woman, have you enlisted these children for the Devil?

TITUBA: No—no, sir, I don't truck with the Devil!

HALE [*of Betty*]: Why can she not wake? Are you silencing this child?

TITUBA: I love me Betty!

HALE: You have sent your spirit out upon this child, have you not? Are you gathering souls for the Devil?

ABIGAIL: She send her spirit on me in *church,* she make me laugh at *prayer!*

PARRIS: She have often laughed at prayer!

ABIGAIL: She comes to me every night to go and drink blood!

TITUBA: You beg *me* to conjure, Abby! She beg *me* make charm—

ABIGAIL: I'll tell you something. She comes to me while I sleep; she's always making me dream corruptions!

TITUBA: Abby!

ABIGAIL: Sometimes I wake and find myself standing in the open doorway and not a stitch on my body! [*Covering herself with her arms, turning up stage and away.*] I always hear her laughing in my sleep. I hear her singing her Barbados songs and tempting me with—

TITUBA: Mister Reverend, I never— ⎱
                                       ⎰ [*Together.*]
HALE: Tituba, I want you to wake ⎱
   this child. ⎰

TITUBA: I have no power on this child, sir.

HALE: You most certainly do, and you will loose her from it now! When did you compact with the Devil?

TITUBA: I don't compact with no Devil!

PARRIS: You will confess yourself or I will take you out and whip you to your death, Tituba!

PUTNAM: This woman must be hanged! She must be taken and hanged!

TITUBA [*kneeling*]: No—no, don't hang Tituba. I tell him I don't desire to work for him, sir.

Act Two not only shows how the court has come into existence: We see how Mary Warren has come to convince herself that she has grounds for denouncing Sarah Good.

MARY: She tried to kill me many times, Goody Proctor!

ELIZABETH: Why, I never heard you mention that before.

MARY [*innocently*]: I never *knew* it before. I never knew anything before. When she come into the court I say to myself, I must not accuse this woman, for she sleep in ditches, and so very old and poor. . . . But then . . . then she sit there, denying and denying, and I feel a misty coldness climbin' up my back, and the skin on my skull begin to creep, and I feel a clamp around my neck and I cannot breathe air; and then . . . [*Entranced, as though it were a miracle.*] I hear a voice, a screamin' voice, and it were *my* voice . . . and all at once I remembered everything she done to me! [*Slight pause as Proctor watches Elizabeth pass him, then speaks, being aware of Elizabeth's alarm.*]

PROCTOR [*looking at Elizabeth*]: Why?—What did she do to you?

MARY [*like one awakened to a marvellous secret insight*]: So many time, Mister Proctor, she come to this very door beggin' bread and a cup of cider—and mark *this*—whenever I turned her away empty—she *mumbled.*

Despite finding the girl unsympathetic, Miller projects himself imaginatively into her mental processes.

In Act Three he uses her again to give a subtle analysis of how she and the others put on a performance of diabolical possession. When she admits that she had only been pretending to faint in the court, Danforth, the judge, counters by asking her to faint now. Like an actress unable to go into an emotional scene without warming up, she cannot. But when, at the end of the act, Abigail fights Proctor's denunciation of her as a whore by staging a new bout of demoniac possession, Mary not only joins in but outscreams the others.

This act also initiates us into the workings and into the psychology of the court itself. Like so many other organizations, it is concerned above all with its own survival and acts most savagely when in danger of being discredited. Miller makes an important point very theatrically when he shows how the prompt arrangements for the arrest of all ninety-one signatories of the petition effectively inhibit anyone of any conscience from producing witnesses in case they too are arrested.

MILLER'S USE OF LANGUAGE

It is a remarkable achievement on Miller's part to write dialogue that is so acceptable as belonging to the seventeenth century and that is so flexible. Sometimes the language is simple and functional; sometimes it is picturesque with images jostling densely against each other. This is Abigail bullying the other girls into submission:

> Now look you. All of you. We danced. And Tituba conjured Ruth Putnam's dead sisters. And that is all. And mark this—let either of you breathe a word, or the edge of a word about the other things, and I will come to you in the black of some terrible night and I will bring a pointy reckoning that will shudder you. And you know I can do it; I saw Indians smash my dear parents' heads on the pillow next to mine, and I have seen some reddish work done at night, and I can make you wish you had never seen the sun go down!

Sexual attraction between Abigail and Proctor is made far more vivid than it is between Chris and Ann in *All My Sons,* partly because of the tension created by Proctor's refusal to give in to his instincts, but mainly because of the language.

> ABIGAIL: I have a sense for heat, John, and yours has drawn me to my window. Do you tell me you've never looked up at my window?
>
> PROCTOR: Perhaps I . . . have.
>
> ABIGAIL: I know you, John, I *know* you. [*She is weeping.*] I cannot sleep for dreamin', I cannot dream but I wake and walk about the house as though I'd find you comin' through some door.
>
> PROCTOR [*taking her hands*]: Child . . .
>
> ABIGAIL [*with a flash of anger. Throwing his hands off*]: How do you call me child!

When he becomes rhetorical as he does when Elizabeth is arrested, the period flavor helps the rhetoric.

> PROCTOR: If *she* is innocent! Why do you never wonder if Parris be innocent, or Abigail? Is the accuser always holy now? Were they born this morning as clean as God's fingers? I'll tell you what's walking Salem—vengeance is walking Salem. We are what we always were in Salem, but now the little crazy children are jangling the keys of the kingdom, and common vengeance writes the law! This warrant's vengeance; I will not give my wife to vengeance!

In the original version of the play, the level of the writing was consistently maintained, but six months after the New York opening, Miller rewrote some of Proctor's part, introducing several rather jarring purple passages. The scene with Elizabeth at the beginning of Act Two suffers and there is a seriously damaging lapse at the end of the play, just after he has torn up his confession. Here is the original version:

> HALE: Man, you will hang!—You cannot!
>
> PROCTOR [*crossing slowly* RIGHT *to Elizabeth, takes her hands for a moment. Simply with dignity*]: Pray God it speaks some goodness for me. [*They embrace. He then holds her at arm's length.*] Give them no tear. Show them a heart of stone and sink them with it.

And here is the rewrite:

> HALE: Man, you will hang! You cannot!
>
> PROCTOR [*his eyes full of tears*]: I can. And there's your first marvel, that I can. You have made your magic now, for now I do think I see some shred of goodness in John Proctor. Not enough to weave a banner with, but white enough to keep it from such dogs. [*Elizabeth, in a burst of terror, rushes to him and weeps against his hand.*] Give them no tear! Tears pleasure them! Show honor now, show a stony heart and sink them with it! [*He has lifted her, and kisses her now with great passion.*]

Another change he made at this time was to cut out the scene in which Proctor and Abigail meet at night in a wood. This came between Elizabeth's arrest and the scene in the anteroom of the court, and it showed Abigail as crazed to the point of believing in her own fiction.

> ABIGAIL: I cannot bear lewd looks no more, John. My spirit's changed entirely. I ought be given Godly looks when I suffer for them as I do.
>
> PROCTOR: Oh? How do you suffer, Abby?
>
> ABIGAIL [*Pulls up dress*]: Why, look at my leg. I'm holes all over from their damned needles and pins. [*Touching her stomach.*] The jab your wife gave me's not healed yet, y'know.
>
> PROCTOR [*seeing her madness now*]: Oh, it isn't.
>
> ABIGAIL: I think sometimes she pricks it open again while I sleep.

This is not altogether satisfactory and it makes us see her behavior in the court in a very different light—as more spontaneous, less calculating. But without this scene, she remains underdeveloped and her disappearance at the end of the play leaves us unsatisfied.

Altogether the end is slightly disappointing, particularly in the new version. Apart from Proctor's rhetoric and Abigail's absence, the focus seems to have narrowed. There are some good touches at the beginning of the act (like the mention of cows wandering through the highroads) to give us an impression of how the whole community has been affected by the wholesale arrests. But afterward the general light on the social background dims down until there seems to be nothing but an individual spotlight on Proctor.

The Crucible's Contemporary Context Is Still Relevant Today

Jeanne-Marie A. Miller

After outlining the major events of America's inglorious hunt for Communists in the 1950s, Jeanne-Marie A. Miller discusses *The Crucible* in its contemporary political and social context. The play depicts the eroding effects of emotional terrorism and the dangers of allowing fear to transform the courts into a travesty of truth and justice. Although the reviews were mixed when the play opened in 1953, Miller suggests that with the McCarthy era slipping into history, the play's broader social message can be appreciated. The play presents a warning that social witch-hunts are still popular in America and that respect for individual rights must be protected and honored.

Jeanne-Marie A. Miller teaches English and American drama at Howard University in Washington, D.C. Her articles have appeared in many periodicals, including the *Journal of Negro Education*, the *CLA Journal*, and the *Journal of Negro History*.

Despite the continued economic decline in America during the Great Depression, Americans, for the most part, remained hostile to the Communist party, although the long crisis did make communism more attractive to some. Many attracted to communism did not join the party, all who joined did not remain members, and not all who wanted to remain members were permitted to do so. Clifford Odets,[1] for example, discontinued his membership in and association with the Communist party when he discovered that the pressures which the party tried to bring to bear upon his writing were stifling to

1. American playwright

Reprinted from "Odets, Miller, and Communism," by Jeanne-Marie A. Miller, *CLA Journal*, vol. 19 (June 1996), pp. 484–93, by permission of the College Language Association.

122

him as an artist. The House Committee on Un-American Activities, headed by Representative Martin Dies, admitted that the greater majority of American people had been immune to both the Nazis and Communists.

In America's recent past, however, an inglorious witch hunt was initiated by several incidents. For example, Alger Hiss was suspected of having been a Communist when employed by the State Department; Klaus Fuchs in England was convicted of revealing atomic secrets to Russia; ten ranking American Communists were convicted under the Smith Act of 1939 of conspiring to overthrow the government. Against this backdrop Senator Joseph R. McCarthy of Wisconsin charged that during "twenty years of treason," the Democrats, under the leadership of Franklin D. Roosevelt and Harry Truman, had "conspired" to deliver America to the "Reds."

> F. D. R. got into World War II mainly to help Russia, gave away everything to Stalin at Yalta; Harry presented China to the Reds and recalled General MacArthur because he was about to beat them; Alger Hisses were concealed in every government office, college, and corporation, ready to take over when Stalin pushed the button.[2]

Efforts were made to remove so-called subversives from the Federal government, colleges, and even businesses. Careers and reputations of thousands were ruined.

As long as McCarthy confined his accusations to professors, scholars, and the foreign service, those Americans who disliked intellectuals and the "white spat boys" did not protest against this demagogue. In 1954, when McCarthy turned his attention to the Protestant clergy and the United States Army, the administration began to take notice. When McCarthy demanded that he be allowed to use the F.B.I. files in order to search for names of new victims, President Dwight D. Eisenhower denounced McCarthy as one who tried "to set himself above the laws of our land" and "to override orders of the President." Although censured by the Senate, McCarthy had succeeded in injecting into the body politic a poisonous suspicion that divided the country.

THE CRUCIBLE AS ALLEGORY

It was during this period of national hysteria and war on social and political heretics that Arthur Miller wrote *The*

---

2. Samuel Eliot Morison, *The Oxford History of the American People* (New York: Oxford University Press, 1965), p. 1,074

Crucible. Ostensibly, Miller's drama is a work about the tragedy of the notorious Salem witchcraft trials. The play, however, is a drama of 1953, the year it was produced, as well as of 1692. *The Crucible*, then, is veiled allegory, but it is not a simple parable.

The play begins slowly with a prologue, an overture, which gives general background, and then gains momentum and power as it progresses. *The Crucible* offers classic examples from history of mass hysteria, epidemic madness, which causes many innocent people to lose their lives. Charged with trafficking with the Devil, these victims were tried and sentenced by people as respectable as themselves, largely on the evidence of young girls who had been caught dancing nude in the moonlight. On another level, Miller is pointing out that witch hunting, with all of its ramifications, is still a popular sport in America.

The emotional terrorism in this four-act drama is initiated by Betty, Reverend Samuel Parris' daughter, Abigail, his teenaged niece, and the other girls who were discovered participating in the nighttime frolic. Because Betty appears to be in a trance from which she cannot be awakened, the Reverend John Hale, a witchcraft specialist from Beverly, has been summoned. The hysteria mounts when Ann Putnam announces that her daughter, too, is ill. Mrs. Putnam attributes to witchcraft her own loss of so many babies shortly after their birth. After the terrified Tituba, Parris' slave, confesses to witchcraft and names two old women as her accomplices, Abigail and Betty add names of other Salemites to the list of the guilty. This action sets in motion the shameful fanaticism in Salem that is now a part of our spotted past.

When the overture ends, the action focuses on John and Elizabeth Proctor, a farming couple, who become the victims of Abigail, who once worked for them as a serving girl. She was dismissed when Elizabeth discovered Abigail's affair with John. The young woman still harbors an affection for John Proctor and eagerly awaits his return to her. Meanwhile Goody Osburn is condemned to be hanged, whereas Sarah Good has saved herself by confessing. Innocent words and actions now are given dark meanings, and a husband's thoughtless statement about his wife's hiding the books she reads is enough to have her charged with witchcraft and arrested. The village oddities are the first to be named, but as the fever spreads, even the worthies are suspected. Rebecca

Nurse is charged with, supernaturally, killing the Putnam infants; Abigail, in seeking revenge, charges Elizabeth Proctor.

In some cases the informer assumes a new role of superiority. For a while Mary Warren, the Proctors' servant, is important. Now an "official of the court," she tells her employer: "The Devil's loose in Salem, Mr. Proctor, we must discover where he's hiding!"

The Reverend Hale offers a reason for the hysteria: "Theology . . . is a fortress; no crack in a fortress may be accounted small." He, at first, approves of the arrests and trusts to the justice of the courts:

> Though our hearts break we cannot flinch; these are new times, sir. There is a misty plot afoot so subtle we should be criminal to cling to old respects and ancient friendships. I have seen too many frightful proofs in court—the Devil is alive in Salem, and we dare not quail to follow, wherever the accusing finger points!

It is left to John Proctor to question the character of the accusers: "Is the accuser always holy now? Were they born this morning as clean as God's fingers?"

BREAKDOWN OF THE LEGAL SYSTEM

The court of justice becomes greatly feared. When the Salem men present an affidavit containing more than ninety signatures, testifying to the immaculateness of the accused wives, the husbands are told that those who signed will be arrested. Mary Warren is so frightened by Abigail in the court that she will not press charges against her as a fraud. The girls with their histrionics—their moaning and screaming—snatch away reputation and life. In this court, spectral evidence is accepted as truth. Here fright makes a travesty of truth and justice.

John Proctor, to discredit Abigail, admits his adultery, but his wife, ignorant of his confession, shields his good name. When Mary Warren accuses Proctor of witchcraft, he, too, is arrested. During his imprisonment Proctor ponders whether or not to confess to a lie to save his life. He gains strength from Rebecca Nurse who, in refusing to confess, resists the prevailing insanity. She, a revered and ancient citizen of Salem, with her soundness of mind contrasts sharply with the hysteria, the suffocating madness, that has gripped Massachusetts and makes clear the absurdity of Salem's witchcraft trials. Finally, Proctor forfeits his life, for he refuses to confess to the false accusations. Thus he is hanged along with the other victims of gross ignorance and militant theology. The play is a tragedy of a whole society.

CRITICAL RESPONSE TO THE PLAY

Many critics were unimpressed with *The Crucible* when it was first produced in 1953. One critic, writing in the *New Republic*, states that the analogy between "red-baiting" and witch hunting seems complete only to Communists. Only to them is the menace of communism as fictitious as the menace of witches.

John Mason Brown, in a favorable review of this drama, sees clearly the parallels between 1692 and 1953:

> We are subject to fears born of the "ideological intensities" of our times. Due to these fears, there are those among us who have "much forgotten what our fathers came in the wilderness to see." Hence the loose charges of Communism, the reckless smearing without proof, and the Salemlike willingness to believe persons guilty before their guilt has been proved.

Our obligation as a people dedicated to freedom, Brown continues, is to protect the innocent while we search for the guilty.

Miller, once called to testify before a Congressional Committee investigating communism in this country, denies that he was "pressing an historical allegory" in *The Crucible.* Because he was impressed by the overwhelming heroism of some of the Salem victims "who displayed an almost frightening personal integrity," it is these victims whom he wished to celebrate and raise out of historic dust. Miller states: "The only sure and valid aim—speaking of art as a weapon—is the humanizing of man."

MILLER'S SOCIAL WARNING

When I saw *The Crucible* in the l960's, I, like many others in the audience, was caught up in the exciting depiction of one of the errors of our past. I, too, was reminded of the mania that swept America in the 1950's when, standing before audiences, the Senator from Wisconsin held in his upraised hand a list of alleged Communists. In the 1960's, however, the "Red Scare" in this land had subsided, and our attention was focused on "containing" communism in other countries, feeding the poor in our own, and defining a phenomenon called "Black Power." Thus the McCarthy era had slipped into our ugly past, and one could evaluate *The Crucible* as art without being distracted by its allegory. Its warning, however, was clear.

Despite the controversy that still rages about *The Crucible*, this drama remains a powerful work, with exciting conflicts and dialogue colored with terms from our colonial past. Miller in this work demands greater respect for the rights of individuals.

Like Odets, with whose work he is familiar, Miller is concerned with social issues affecting contemporary society. Like Odets, he is the possessor of a bold and sensitive social conscience. Both playwrights, affected by the political and social currents of their times, dared to dramatize these currents and, at the same time, deliver a warning to the American people.

The Universal Appeal of *The Crucible*

John H. Ferres

Although the witch-hunts of *The Crucible* parallel
Joseph McCarthy's hunts for Communists in the
United States in the 1950s, John H. Ferres explains
that the play moves beyond these historical events and
explores universal issues that resonate with contemporary audiences. Ferres argues that the play's appeal
is founded on the concept that individuals must tear
away the disguises that society forces them to wear
and confront the essential truth about themselves, no
matter the odds or consequences. To do this requires
individual dissent against the irrational and destructive authority that frequently governs modern life.

According to Ferres, *The Crucible* draws on universal conflicts that are as old as organized society: dissent versus authority, fear versus courage, evil versus
goodness, and the individual versus society. In short,
The Crucible is a timeless play that deals artistically
with the human condition.

John H. Ferres is a professor of American thought
and language at Michigan State University, East
Lansing. He is the author of *Arthur Miller: A Reference Guide* and *Modern Commonwealth Literature.*

To many in the audience at the Martin Beck Theater in New
York where it opened on January 22, 1953, *The Crucible* seemed
to draw a parallel between the Salem witch trials of 1692 and
government investigations of alleged Communist subversion in
this country in the late 1940s and early 1950s. Given the national temper at the time, this is hardly surprising. [American
drama critic] Henry Popkin reminds us that for several years before *The Crucible* was produced "public investigations had been
examining and interrogating radicals, former radicals, and

possible former radicals, requiring witnesses to tell about others and not only about themselves. The House Committee [on] Un-American Activities evolved a memorable and much-quoted sentence: 'Are you now, or have you ever been, a member of the Communist party?' Borrowing a phrase from a popular radio program, its interrogators called it 'the $64 question.'"

Far from denying the parallel, Miller has emphasized it repeatedly in the interpolated commentary on *The Crucible*, in the introduction to the *Collected Plays*, and elsewhere, while insisting at the same time that he was really concerned with what lay behind the historical phenomena:

> It was not only the rise of "McCarthyism" that moved me, but some thing much more weird and mysterious. It was the fact that a political, objective, knowledgeable campaign from the far Right was capable of creating not only a terror, but a new subjective reality, a veritable mystique which was gradually assuming even a holy resonance. The wonder of it all struck me that so picayune a cause, carried forward by such manifestly ridiculous men, should be capable of paralyzing thought itself.... Astounded, I watched men pass me by without a nod whom I had known rather well for years; and again, the astonishment was produced by my knowledge ... that the terror in these people was being knowingly planned and consciously engineered, and yet all they knew was terror.... There was a new religiosity in the air, not merely the kind expressed by the spurt in church construction and church attendance, but an official piety which my reading of American history could not reconcile with the free-wheeling iconoclasm of the country's past. I saw forming a kind of interior mechanism of confession and forgiveness of sins which until now had not been rightly categorized as sins. New sins were being created monthly. It was very odd how quickly these were accepted into the new orthodoxy, quite as though they had been there since the beginning of time.... I saw accepted the notion that conscience was no longer a private matter but one of state administration. I saw men handing conscience to other men and thanking other men for the opportunity of doing so.

Later he was to write, "I thought then that in terms of this process the witch-hunts had something to say to the anti-Communist hysteria."

Miller has attributed *The Crucible*'s relatively brief initial Broadway run of six months—*Death of a Salesman* ran for over eighteen—to the reviewers' dismissal of the play "as a cold, anti-McCarthy tract." But with the exception of Brooks Atkinson and Walter Kerr, the newspaper reviewers either denied or chose to ignore the contemporary parallels, while generally praising the play itself. Eric Bentley claimed that Miller had overlooked the crucial point that Communism, as distinct from witchcraft, does in fact exist, but praised his ability as a playwright. On the other hand, some reviewers had as many reservations about that ability as they did about the parallel with McCarthyism. The first act was too diffuse, they said; or the treatment of plot was too conventional after *Death of a Salesman.* A few years later the play was revived off-Broadway, where it ran for over 500 performances to much more certain acclaim, and since then it has been in almost continuous production in this country and abroad. It held the stage for several seasons in France and has found a permanent place in the repertories of such illustrious companies as Sir Laurence Olivier's National Theater in Great Britain. Next to *Death of a Salesman,* it remains Miller's most popular play in both the theater and the classroom.

CONTEMPORARY APPEAL OF *THE CRUCIBLE*

The contemporary appeal of *The Crucible* can hardly be attributed to any analogy it draws between the Salem witch-hunts of 1692 and Joe McCarthy's Communist hunts, however, since the majority of those who see or read the play today are probably too young to remember the Wisconsin senator. Foreign audiences must be even less conscious of the analogy. Why then has *The Crucible* held up so well? What makes it still worth reading and performing? One can perhaps begin to answer these questions by quoting something that Miller said in an interview about his later play, *After the Fall*: "I am trying to define what a human being should be, how he can survive in today's society without having to appear to be a different person from what he basically is." Despite its seventeenth-century setting, he might have been talking about a central theme of *The Crucible,* not only for audiences of the McCarthy years but for those of today as well. Certainly the play more than bears out Miller's belief that drama is "the art of the present tense."

To put it simply, Miller believes a man must be true to himself and to his fellows, even though being untrue may be the only way to stay alive. Out of the ordeal of his personal crucible, each of the principal characters comes to know the truth about himself. In order to confront his essential self, to discover that self in the void between being and seeming, a man must strip away the disguises society requires him to wear. John Proctor, refusing at the moment of truth to sell his friends, tears up his confession. Making a comparable decision, a character in *After the Fall* says, "Everything kind of falls away, excepting—one's self. One's truth." Once the self has been revealed by this process, a man must be true to it. Much more than Proctor's era or the Cold War period, ours is a time when traditional values are eroding. The individual feels compelled to look inward for new ones. A man must either stand or fall alone once the fog of old standards has been burned away in the crucible of crisis. Stand or fall, though, he can achieve wholeness of being or "a sense of personal inviolability," in Miller's words, that justifies new faith in himself.

The possibility of genuine self-awareness is a remote one for most people today—not so much because few are tested as Miller's characters are, but because few, to paraphrase Thoreau, are able to live deliberately and confront the essential facts of life. The concern of writers with the loss of the self in modern society has given rise to a whole literature of existential search for identity. It is precisely his identity, his "name," that Proctor will not surrender. The size, complexity, and diversity of our urban technological civilization, in alliance with Madison Avenue techniques for manipulating the mind and stereotyping the personality to a collection of consumer wants, make it difficult to identify the essential self beneath the layers of pseudoself. The real measure of Proctor's heroism as a standard for today lies in his ultimate discovery that life is not worth living if it must be preserved by lies told to one's self and one's friends.

PROCTOR'S SPIRIT OF DISSENT

Since self-understanding implies dissent, the spirit of dissent is strong in *The Crucible*, as strong perhaps as it was among the original Puritans. In the play, the word *authority* always means authority without inner sanction and always implies skepticism. Whether it ought to or not, Proctor's "I like not the smell of this 'authority'" strikes a responsive chord at present. The struggle of Proctor and the others against the theocracy's repressive, irrational, and destructive use of authority is not without parallel in times more recent than the early 1950s. Proctor's gradual rejection of it is a paradigm of the intellectual misgivings of many today. He is shown first to be merely independent-minded about going to church. His excuse is that he needs the extra workday if his farm is to produce to capacity. We learn next that the real reason is his resentment of the Reverend Mr. Parris' grasping materialism, hypocritically concealed behind a façade of piety, and also his preoccupation with his congregation's possible future in hell instead of its actual spiritual needs in the present. Although Proctor has never "desired the destruction of religion," he can "see no light of God" in Parris and is "sick of Hell." His disillusionment is not complete, however, until he is arrested for witchcraft. At that point he is convinced that "God is dead!"

If not dead, then certainly He has withdrawn His blessing from a system engaged in persecutions worse than the Anglican Church's persecution of the Pilgrims, from which they had sought refuge in the New World. Like many revolutionaries and reactionaries today, Danforth and Hathorne are convinced that since their cause—the extirpation of Satan and all his works from the new Canaan—is right and just, any means is justifiable in serving that end. Freedom of thought and expression, as well as a man's right to a fair trial, may therefore be denied, with the judges abrogating the most common-sense rules of evidence while they intimidate the community into accepting their self-serving view of justice. Proctor's questions, "Is the accuser always holy now?" and "Is every defense an attack upon the court?" are met by Danforth's "I cannot pardon these when twelve are already hanged for the same crime." Proctor is indeed attacking the court, and perhaps the whole system it represents, but his protest ends in frustration and what amounts to suicide because the court itself insists on arbitrating the dispute.

Proctor rebels against the essentially totalitarian view of society that Danforth and Hathorne uphold. It is the view that the state knows best how a man should think and act. Carried to its extreme, as it was in the witchcraft trials, it bears out Nietzsche's[1] dictum that the basis of society is the rationalization of cruelty. Proctor represents the view of society held by the Enlightenment thinkers—that society should be founded on the common good, as agreed upon by all reasonable men. This may be seen in his attitude toward adultery with Abigail. He feels guilt not so much because the Church has decreed adultery a sin as because it goes against "his own vision of decent conduct." Rather than an oppressively paternal state pre-

1. German philosopher Friedrich

scribing what he does, man needs a community whose essence is human, with friends who share common goals and beliefs. The witch trials demonstrate that the theocracy in effect suppresses the growth of such a community by inducing and finally forcing people to betray one another.

THE CONFLICT BETWEEN MYSTERY AND RATIONALISM

The position of the theocracy in 1692 was that witchcraft was both a sin and a crime, albeit an invisible one. Its very invisibility, however, showed it to be a phenomenon of great mystery and, as such, best dealt with by those qualified to deal with mysteries—namely, the civil and ecclesiastical officers of the theocracy. The Proctors, and finally Hale, want no part of mystery when a man is on trial for his life. Nevertheless, Americans are a people whose religious roots bind them to a belief in mystery. They are also a people whose traditions, both secular and religious, bind them to a belief in rationalism. Miller believes the American audience will side with Proctor in his encounter with Hale in Act I. When Hale arrives in Salem with armfuls of books on witchcraft, Parris takes some and remarks on how heavy they are. To Hale's reply that they are "weighted with authority," Proctor says that he has heard Hale is "a sensible man" and hopes he will leave some sense in Salem. The Puritans were the first Americans to experience our characteristic equivocation between belief in mystery, or myth, and faith in nonmystery, or rationalism. Dedicated by an unworldly religion to a life of self-denial and self-restraint as preparation for the mystery of heavenly salvation, they found themselves in a land eager to reward then and there material ambitions and appetites that were quite unmysterious in origin. Proctor, as noted earlier, cannot pass up the chance to get in an extra day's plowing on Sunday— any more than he can forgo his opportunity with Abigail.

The Salem episode can be seen as the inevitable explosion of a social schizophrenia suppressed for sixty years. To the extent that this condition was the product of real or imagined threats from outside the Puritan enclave, war with the pagan Indians or the French Papists might have been the result. But in fact the Salemite found exorcism of his schizophrenia in the hysteria of the witch trials and the sacrifice of the scapegoat victims. The Reverend Mr. Hale, comprehending at last the enormity of the witch trials, denounces them at the same moment that Proctor concludes God is dead. A churchman in conflict with the Church, a convert to humanism opposed to all he once epitomized, Hale denounces the theocratic system. Faced with a Church that will hang a person on the strength of a controversial passage of Scripture, Hale concludes that "Life . . . is God's most precious gift; no principle, however glorious, may justify the taking of it." One of these scriptural principles was the charitable obligation of each Christian to be his brother's keeper, a principle that in 1692 had been perverted to sanction malicious gossip and informing. If the witch trials marked the end of the theocracy's power in Massachusetts, it was because the theocracy had ossified into a monument to dead ideas as far as the John Proctors were concerned. As Miller notes, "the time of the armed camp had almost passed, and since the country was reasonably— although not wholly—safe, the old disciplines were beginning to rankle." In the play, the failure of the parents to see through the children's pretense of witchcraft is consistently ludicrous until it becomes tragic. Expecting children to behave as adults, the Puritans nevertheless refused to respect them as adults. In this way they assured rebellion against their authority, whether in the form of a childish prank that gets tragically out of hand, or the plain refusal of a Mary Warren to stand for whippings and being ordered to bed. "I am eighteen and a woman," she says.

It must be said, in extenuation perhaps, that the Puritans believed in witchcraft much more firmly than they understood the natural penchant for mischief of the young, which could also be assigned to a diabolical source. Even had they understood, doubtless they would have felt that to dismiss the phenomenon before their eyes as a childish prank was exactly what Satan wanted them to do. They had no knowledge of child psychology, much less the psychology of hysteria. Rebecca Nurse is the only one to state what seems so obvious to us, but no one listens. A mother of eleven children, Rebecca has "seen them all through their silly seasons, and when it comes on them they will run the Devil bowlegged keeping up with their mischief. . . . A child's spirit is like a child, you can never catch it by running after it; you must stand still, and, for love, it will soon itself come back."

UNIVERSAL APPEAL OF *THE CRUCIBLE*

Part of the contemporaneity of *The Crucible* lies in its universality. The right of dissent versus the claims of authority

makes up a conflict as old as organized society. Both Sophocles' *Antigone* and Shaw's *Joan of Arc* afford parallels to *The
Crucible* in this connection. Names like Roger Williams, Anne
Hutchinson, Henry David Thoreau, Martin Luther King, and
indeed the whole tradition of minority dissent in America
come to mind. The witch trials confront the mind with another age-old question too: how should we respond to evil?
And its equally ancient corollary: what if the evil lie in us?
Writing about *The Crucible* in 1967, Miller said:

> No man lives who has not got a panic button and when it is
> pressed by the clean white hand of moral duty, a certain mur-
> derous train is set in motion. Socially speaking, this is what the
> play is and was "about," and it is this which I believe makes it
> survive long after the political circumstances of its birth have
> evaporated in the public mind. [This] tragic process underlying
> the political manifestation [is] as much a part of humanity as
> walls and food and death, and no play will make it go away.
> When irrational terror takes to itself the fiat of moral goodness,
> somebody has to die.

A susceptibility to paranoid fear is often the root of human
tragedy, whether manifested in the slaughter of the Biblical
innocents or in the internment of one hundred thousand
Japanese-American citizens during World War II. In other
words, if *The Crucible* is a social play, it applies to all societies
rather than to any particular one. The setting of 1692 and the
sociopolitical climate of 1953 take on the quality of timeless-
ness found in Greek or Shakespearean tragedy. The persecution of both periods becomes the persecution of any period.
But although Miller is careful to show how personal interest
can infect society, the play seems less concerned now with a
social condition than with a moral dilemma that continues to
be part of the human condition for each one of us. In the same
way, perhaps, *King Lear* is not, at least for modern readers, a
tragedy about the social, much less the cosmic, effects of a
king's misrule, but rather about the personal consequences of
an old man's perversity for himself and his immediate circle.

For Americans, the play has something additional to offer
in reminding us of our still potent Puritan legacy. It is a legacy
larger in its effects than ever before because of the growth of
America since the date of inheritance, although the passage of
time has made it harder to recognize. As Miller points out, the
Puritans believed that as God's chosen people they held "the
candle that would light the world," and our inheritance of
their belief has both "helped and hurt us." It provided much

of the zeal and discipline necessary to civilize a new land and eventually make it into a Christian nation. It also degenerated into the imperialism of the Manifest Destiny doctrine in the nineteenth century in the same way that a crusade against Communism has degenerated, in the view of many, into military aggrandizement in this century. Danforth's black-and-white edict that one is "either with this court or he must be counted against it" is not very remote from either the continuing tendency of the conservative mind to regard foreign and domestic attempts at radical social transformation as conceived in Communism and born to subvert democracy, or the contrary tendency of the radical mind to suppose that to it alone has been vouchsafed the revelation of political and moral truth. If the use of violence is any indication, the Puritan psychology of terror is a national obsession that grows each year.

Miller's Contribution to American Theater

Richard Watts Jr.

Richard Watts Jr. suggests that when *The Crucible* opened, its parallels to the McCarthy hearings distracted critics and theatergoers from appreciating its dramatic quality and led them to criticize the play as merely a staged political tract. With time, however, as the McCarthy phenomenon recedes into the past, the play can be enjoyed for its inherent and enduring dramatic power.

Watts names Arthur Miller, Tennessee Williams, and William Inge as the most influential playwrights in postwar American drama. Of the three, Miller stands out as America's most important social dramatist. According to Watts, Miller is a moralist whose plays philosophically attack weaknesses in American society. Miller's broad appeal as a playwright stems from his desire to assess the state of the world rather than indulge in self-centered emotional analysis. Watts also argues that *The Crucible* draws large audiences because of its straightforward narrative, its honest treatment of theme, and its development of characters who, although they may lack completely rounded proportions, are nevertheless dramatically effective.

Richard Watts Jr. worked for forty years as a journalist and drama critic for the *New York Herald-Tribune* and *New York Post*.

"The Crucible" is that rarity in the American theatre, a play which seems finer and more alive today than when it was first produced, in this case 1953. The phenomenon isn't unique, but how unusual and cheering it is can probably be appreciated only by the veteran drama-lover, whose memories are sure to be filled with works he had cherished, only to find in some later revival that they have lost their savor. And what makes the case of "The Crucible" even more gratifying is that, despite its setting of the Salem witch trials toward the end of the seventeenth century, it was essentially a topical drama, the sort which is generally regarded as becoming outmoded most quickly and emphatically.

Considering the date of its writing and first production, which was that of the period of national hysteria and war on social and political heretics that gave a Wisconsin politician named McCarthy his claim to an ugly footnote in history, it was inevitable that a play dealing with a notorious earlier epoch of American hysteria should carry its overtones of contemporary significance. It was even more certain when the dramatist was Arthur Miller, the proud possessor of a bold and sensitive social conscience. The modern comparisons are present only implicitly, but they are proudly there.

Yet somehow they tended to be harmful to "The Crucible" as a play in 1953, even though their courageous fighting spirit gave it a kind of lofty dignity that was impressive and admirable. But even many of those who were entirely on the dramatist's side, and hailed him for the stand he took, were not without their reservations about what he had written. The contemporary parallels did have a way of distorting, certainly not the truth but the dramatic values, because they distracted one's attention by getting in the way of the story, instead of underlining it, and reminding the spectator almost as frequently of the differences in the two eras as of the shocking similarities.

Today, with the nightmare era of McCarthy moving farther into the past, those particular details are no longer of distracting importance, although the general issue of freedom of judgment opposed to the brutal domination of intolerance remains as great as ever. And, with nothing to distract the attention by forcing on it those parallels with one especial case of national yielding to the hysteria of witch-hunting, "The Crucible" can be judged for what it is, a moving drama about the personal tragedy of the notorious Salem trials which makes by implication an eloquent case on the universal subject of intolerance using trumped-up hysteria for its evil purposes.

It represents quite a victory for Mr. Miller that his play should grow in stature with the passing of time. For it is now clear that "The Crucible" was another victim of a sinister epoch in our history. It isn't that the play has improved, but that the atmosphere surrounding it has. It was judged as a kind of political pamphlet for the stage, when it was actually a work of dramatic art all the time. When Mr. Miller felt that it was underrated on the occasion of its first presentation, he was partially to blame by being so frank about its editorial viewpoint, but he was right about its quality.

It may be worth saying parenthetically on behalf of the critics and paying theatregoers who were a trifle chill to the play when they saw it in 1953 and expressed enthusiasm when they looked at it again in 1957 that neither they nor the days of their first attendance were entirely at fault. In large part, the change in verdict was due to the odd fact that the original Broadway production, with a cast of prominent actors, was inferior to the off-Broadway revival, which had a cast of virtually unknown players. But that is a matter of perhaps merely academic interest. The important thing is that, as the reader may find for himself, "The Crucible" is a play worthy of its author.

MILLER'S STATUS IN AMERICAN THEATRE

As for the current status of Arthur Miller in the American theatre, it is stating an accepted fact to say that he, Tennessee Williams and William Inge are the living American dramatists who stand out pre-eminently. Since the death of Eugene O'Neill, it is they who have given our stage its chief dignity and importance in the eyes of not only their fellow countrymen but of the world. In addition to their standing at the head of their class, the Big Three of our post-war drama have at least one other thing in common. Their vision of existence is a gloomy one. This tendency toward philosophical sadness has caused a number of people, chiefly in this country, to complain that they are lacking in the spirit of good, old-fashioned American optimism, an objection which blithely ignores the inescapable fact that such indigenously American authors as Melville, Poe, Hawthorne and O'Neill were likewise apostles of philosophical gloom. Miller, Williams and Inge are clearly in an entirely respectable national tradition.

Being a playwright who has a definite way of doing things in the theatre, Mr. Miller not unexpectedly is said to find the lack of interest in contemporary social problems and their concentration on subjective concerns in the plays of Tennessee Williams and William Inge a weakness in their work. It is natural that he should. A creative writer of the strong convictions necessary for important achievements is bound to feel intensely that his approach to artistic creation is the only correct one. The chances are that the Messrs. Williams and Inge believe their individual approaches are what Mr. Miller needs. Since a diversity of visions and approaches is necessary to a properly diversified theatre, it would be a shame if they tried the same road, but it is right that each should be convinced that his way is the soundest. It is, for him.

As matters stand, Mr. Miller is our one important social dramatist, now that Lillian Hellman appears to be devoting her time to adaptations and Clifford Odets is a screen writer in Hollywood. It is my impression that Miller lacks something of Miss Hellman's gift for dramatic fireworks and Mr. Odets' capacity to give a touch of poetry to his realistic prose. On the other hand, he has, I think, a mind that broods over the state of the world and over moral concerns more philosophically, more compassionately and less dogmatically. He gives the impression of being a man who is earnestly striving to find his way through a world beset by moral difficulties, and the results of his pilgrimage can be very stirring.

MILLER AS MORALIST

He is essentially a moralist, which makes the charge that he is some kind of orthodox left-wing economic determinist seem disproved immediately. The problems faced in his plays are invariably moral problems. As a social dramatist, Mr. Miller is concerned with analyzing the quality of contemporary American civilization, and he can be deeply critical of it. But the weaknesses he finds are moral weaknesses. In his "Death of a Salesman," which is one of the most important plays ever written in this country, the essential tragedy of the central figure was, not his failure in business or his discovery of the arrival of old age, but his surrender to false ideals of success. His other troubles were important chiefly because they enabled him to recognize his basic failure.

Being preoccupied with the moral problems of modern American society, Mr. Miller inevitably still had them in mind when he wrote his play about seventeenth century Salem. He was interested in something that had shocked his moral sense, the weakness in the national character that made a people presumably dedicated to a belief in freedom and the right of dissent so susceptible to hysterical violence against dissenters and heretics. The frightening thing was happening at the time he wrote, and he turned to a famous period in our early annals, which appeared to have so many parallels to the current frenzy and from which contemporary lessons might be drawn.

Granting that the similarities were undoubtedly many, there were also those differences. For one matter, the danger from Russian subversion was a more believable menace than the witch cults of pioneer Massachusetts. Delving for a moment into the paradox known as constructive criticism, "The Crucible" might have proved more effective in 1953 if the playwright had acknowledged that there was a witch cult in the seventeenth century which gave plausibility to the wild and evil charges against innocent people. Anyway, the fact that there were differences as well as similarities in the two periods did get in the way of a proper appreciation of a powerful and disturbing drama.

Such a difficulty happily doesn't interfere with the play's effectiveness today. The basic issues of emotional terrorism and the endless struggle between the rights of free men and mass efforts to destroy them under the guise of defending decency and right-mindedness being still with us, "The Crucible," unhampered by distracting topical questions, stands forth as an eloquent statement on the universal subject of the free man's courageous and never-ending fight against mass pressures to make him bow down in conformity.

MILLER'S POWER AS A DRAMATIST

Only someone who had neither seen nor read a play by Arthur Miller could imagine that, because "The Crucible" is a polemic, it might be cold, bloodless and unemotional as a drama. For one of his most notable qualities as a playwright is his ability to say what he has to say with narrative skill and vigorous dramatic power. It may be in part because he is so much less concerned with subjective brooding and emotional self-analysis than with the setting down of objective events, with contemplating the state of the world and not the state of his own subconsciousness, that his plays, even his less satisfying ones, have such straightforward theatrical forcefulness.

Whether or not this is the chief reason, it is a fact that he has the rare ability to write tragedies for extroverts, who are not ordinarily the people one expects to appreciate tragedy. This was particularly the case with "Death of a Salesman," and must have had much to do with its popular success. But I was convinced of this through considerable cross-examining of many playgoing friends and acquaintances, with the curious discovery of a new law of inverse proportions. The less introverted they were, the more they were emotionally overwhelmed by the tragedy of Willie Loman, the doomed salesman.

There was another odd thing about the appeal of "Death of a Salesman." It is an accepted fact that women make up the bulk of the audiences at serious plays, and this wasn't changed at Mr. Miller's drama. But it was true that men constituted a larger proportion of the audience attending it than at virtually any other tragedy known to box offices, and that it was the men who, instead of attending to drag their wives away at the end of the first act, stayed on enthralled to find themselves caught up in the meaning of the play.

It would be impossible to make any similar suggestion about the appeal of "The Crucible." But it seems to me that the same quality of frank theatrical impact and concern with straightforward narrative interest that gave "Death of a Salesman" a far larger audience success than we have come to expect of plays with tragic themes, has much to do with the popular appeal of "The Crucible." It would be wildly unfair to suggest that Mr. Miller is a conscious showman in this respect, shrewdly putting in spectator values to stir up business at the box office. He is clearly too conscientious an artist for that, and he certainly never softens the stern honesty of his theme and viewpoint. But he also happens to have a gift for sheer dramatic effect, and it serves him admirably.

This isn't to say that "The Crucible" is without its weaknesses. Its opening exposition seems to me a little cluttered and clouded, and it takes a bit of time before the situation of the frightened girls is made clear. And the play has some of the defects of its virtues. The straightforwardness of the narrative and the viewpoint, once the exposition is out of the way, tends to oversimplify the conflict and make the characters representing good and evil seem dramatized points of view rather than full-length, fully-rounded human beings.

It might be argued, though, that this is really not a criticism of the drama but a description of the sort of drama it is. Despite its realistic form, "The Crucible" is less dramatic realism than a modern morality play, in which the characters are intended to be dramatized symbols of good and evil. My only reason for doubt, probably an unfair one to Mr.

YOUNG AUDIENCES APPRECIATE *THE CRUCIBLE*

In 1979 editor James J. Martine asked Arthur Miller if he remained prouder of The Crucible *than his other works.*

QUESTION: In 1967, you were prouder of *The Crucible* than anything else you had written. Does that remain so a decade later?

MILLER: I'll tell you about *The Crucible;* first of all, it's the most produced of my plays, more than *Salesman* or anything else. I'm proud of it in the sense that it seems to reach the young very well. They do it all over the place. And I get very moving letters from them sometimes about where it has sent their minds in relation to liberty, in relation to the rights of people. It seems to affect their living as citizens. Which is terrific. And I kind of feel proud about that. They're stronger in their belief in the best things in America because of that.

Matthew C. Roudané, ed., *Conversations with Arthur Miller.* Jackson: University Press of Mississippi, 1987.

Miller, is that Shaw was even more devastating about intolerance in "Saint Joan" by giving its representatives a sound, logical case and making them good and conscientious men, and then showing the horrifying results of what they did. I say this may be unfair to Mr. Miller, but it is also a justified tribute to him that he deserves to be judged by comparison with such a giant as Shaw.

Certainly, too, the characters in his play make up in theatrical vividness for what they may lack in completely rounded proportions. And "The Crucible" is filled with dramatically effective figures. Take just one of them, the conniving girl named Abigail, who is largely responsible for starting the hysteria. She comes close to being a villainess out of melodrama, but, in her evil little way, she is a remarkably fascinating creature. Yet she is not one of his characters to whom Mr. Miller devotes most of his attention. And I doubt if there is a figure in the entire play that doesn't come to striking theatrical life.

Although the actual amount of Arthur Miller's writing for the stage is not large, no one seems to doubt any more that he is one of the most important of contemporary dramatists. And, now that he has become a recognized figure of world dramatic literature, his plays are as familiar in production to the playgoers of Europe as to ours. As a dramatist and a moral force speaking for the conscience of America, he is well represented in "The Crucible."

Arthur Miller's Innocence

Eric Bentley

In a review written shortly after *The Crucible*
opened in 1953, Eric Bentley discusses some of the
play's major weaknesses: The characters lack
development, the lines lack fluidity, and, although
Miller strives for poetry, the play lacks a lyrical quality. Moreover, Bentley suggests that the inevitable
comparison of the Salem trials to the McCarthy hearings lacks meaning because, unlike the witches,
communism is a real and potentially dangerous
threat to society.

Bentley argues that because of Miller's liberalism,
manifest in his social indignation, he presents only
two options, guilt and innocence, making his play
melodramatic. Bentley contends that Miller's villains
are too black and his heroes are too white. Proctor,
for example, has weaknesses but no faults; his
innocence is total.

Eric Bentley (b. 1916) was the drama critic of
The New Republic when he reviewed *The Crucible*,
and his reviews were reprinted in two books, *The
Dramatic Event* and *What is Theatre?* He wrote on
Miller again in *Thinking about the Playwright*, 1987.
Later, he was better known as a playwright, and as
such was inducted into the Theatre Hall of Fame in
1998.

The theatre is provincial. Few events on Broadway have any
importance whatsoever except to that small section of the
community—neither an elite nor a cross section—that sees
Broadway plays. A play by an Arthur Miller or a Tennessee
Williams is an exception. Such a play is not only better than the
majority; it belongs in the mainstream of our culture. Such an

Adapted from "The Innocence of Arthur Miller," by Eric Bentley, in *What Is Theatre?
Incorporating "The Dramatic Event" and Other Reviews,* by Eric Bentley (New York:
Limelight Editions, 1984), by permission of the author. Copyright © Eric Bentley.

author has something to say about America that is worth discussing. In *The Crucible*, Mr. Miller says something that *has* to be discussed. Nor am I limiting my interest to the intellectual sphere. One sits before this play with anything but intellectual detachment. At a moment when we are all being "investigated," or imagining that we shall be, it is vastly disturbing to see indignant images of investigation on the other side of the footlights. Why, one wonders, aren't there dozens of plays each season offering such a critical account of the state of the nation—critical and *engagé*? The appearance of one such play by an author, like Mr. Miller, who is neither an infant, a fool, or a swindler, is enough to bring tears to the eyes.

"Great stones they lay upon his chest until he plead aye or nay. They say he give them but two words. 'More weight,' he says, and died." Mr. Miller's material is magnificent for narrative, poetry, drama. The fact that we sense its magnificence suggests that either he or his actors have in part realized it, yet our moments of emotion only make us the more aware of half-hours of indifference or dissatisfaction. For this is a story not quite told, a drama not quite realized. Pygmalion has labored hard at his statue and it has not come to life. There is a terrible inertness about the play. The individual characters, like the individual lines, lack fluidity and grace. There is an O'Neill-like striving after a poetry and an eloquence which the author does not achieve. "From Aeschylus to Arthur Miller," say the textbooks. The world has made this author important before he has made himself great; perhaps the reversal of the natural order of things weighs heavily upon him. It would be all too easy, script in hand, to point to weak spots. The inadequacy of particular lines, and characters, is of less interest, however, than the mentality from which they come. It is the mentality of the unreconstructed liberal.

There has been some debate as to whether this story of seventeenth-century Salem "really" refers to our current "witch hunt" yet since no one is interested in anything *but* this reference, I pass on to the real point at issue, which is: the validity of the parallel. It is true in that people today are being persecuted on quite chimerical grounds. It is untrue in that communism is not, to put it mildly, merely a chimera. The word communism is used to cover, first, the politics of Marx, second, the politics of the Soviet Union, and, third, the activities of all liberals as they seem to illiberal illiterates. Since Mr. Miller's argument bears only on the third use of the word, its scope is

THE CRUCIBLE'S INITIAL CRITICAL RECEPTION
In a 1985 interview Matthew C. Roudané asked Arthur Miller to respond to the cold reception that The Crucible *received when it premiered in 1953.*

When *The Crucible* opened, we were at the height of the McCarthy period. There was simply a lot of fear and suspicion in the audience. This has been said a thousand times; you know the story I'm sure. It was in many ways a disembodied theater. There was a fear of fear. Once they caught on to what *The Crucible* was about, a coat of ice formed over the audience because they felt they were being called upon to believe something which the reigning powers at the time told them they were not to believe. They would have to disobey very important social commands in order to believe in this play. Consequently the critics, who are merely registering their moment and, with few honorable exceptions have no real independence from it, thought of *The Crucible* as a cold play. Now anyone who's seen *The Crucible* can level criticism, but that surely isn't a legitimate one anymore. It's that *they* felt cold; they were refrigerated by the social climate of that moment. I stood in the back of that theater after opening night and I saw people come by me whom I'd known for years—and wouldn't say hello to me. They were in dread that they would be identified with *me.* Because what I was saying in the play was that a species of hysteria had overtaken the United States and would end up killing people if it weren't recognized. Two years passed. Senator McCarthy died, the pendulum swung, and people began to recognize that he had been a malevolent influence.

Matthew C. Roudané, ed., *Conversations with Arthur Miller.* Jackson: University Press of Mississippi, 1987.

limited. Indeed, the analogy between "red-baiting" and witch hunting can seem complete only to communists, for only to them is the menace of communism as fictitious as the menace of witches. The non-communist will look for certain reservations and provisos. In *The Crucible*, there are none.

To accuse Mr. Miller of communism would of course be to fall into the trap of over-simplification which he himself has set. For all I know he may hate the Soviet state with all the ardor of Eisenhower. What I am maintaining is that his view of life is dictated by assumptions which liberals have to unlearn and which many liberals have rather publicly unlearned. Chief among these assumptions is that of general innocence. In Hebrew mythology, innocence was lost at the very beginning of things; in liberal, especially American liberal, folk-lore, it has not been lost yet; Arthur Miller is the playwright of American liberal folklore. It is as if the merely negative, and legal, definition of innocence were extended to the rest of life: you are innocent until proved guilty, you are innocent if you "didn't do it." Writers have a sort of double innocence: not only can they create innocent characters, they can also write from the viewpoint of innocence—we can speak today not only of the "omniscient" author but of the "guiltless" one.

Such indeed is the viewpoint of the dramatist of indignation, like Miss Hellman or Mr. Miller. And it follows that their plays are melodrama—a conflict between the wholly guilty and the wholly innocent. For a long time liberals were afraid to criti-cize the mentality behind this melodrama because they feared association with the guilty ("harboring reactionary sympa-thies"). But, though a more enlightened view would enjoin as-sociation with the guilty in the admission of a common hu-manity, it does not ask us to underestimate the guilt or to refuse to see "who done it." The guilty men are as black with guilt as Mr. Miller says—what we must ask is whether the in-nocent are as white with innocence. The drama of indignation is melodramatic not so much because it paints its villains too black as because it paints its heroes too white. Othello is not a melodrama, because, though its villain is wholly evil, its hero is not wholly virtuous. *The Crucible* is a melodrama because, though the hero has weaknesses, he has no faults.[1] His inno-cence is unreal because it is total. His author has equipped him with what we might call Super-innocence, for the crime he is accused of not only hasn't been committed by him, it isn't even a possibility: it is the fiction of traffic with the devil. It goes without saying that the hero has all the minor accoutrements of innocence too: he belongs to the right social class (yeoman farmer), does the right kind of work (manual), and, somewhat contrary to historical probability, has the right philosophy (a distinct leaning towards skeptical empiricism). . . .

The innocence of his author is known to us from life as well as art. [American stage director] Elia Kazan made a pub-lic confession of having been a communist and, while doing so, mentioned the names of several of his former comrades. Mr. Miller then brought out a play about an accused man who refuses to name comrades (who indeed dies rather than make a confession at all), and of course decided to end his collaboration with the director who did so much to make him famous. The play has been directed by Jed Harris.

I think there is as much drama in this bit of history as in any Salem witch hunt. The "guilty" director was rejected. An "innocent" one was chosen in his place. There are two stories in this. The first derives from the fact that the better fellow (assuming, for the purpose of argument, that Mr. Harris is the better fellow) is not always the better worker. The awkwardness I find in Mr. Miller's script is duplicated in Mr. Harris's directing. Mr. Kazan would have taken this script up like clay and remolded it. He would have struck fire from the individual actor, and he would have brought one actor into much livelier relationship with another. (Arthur Kennedy is not used up to half his full strength in this production; E.G. Marshall and Walter Hampden give fine performances but each in his own way, Mr. Hampden's way being a little too English, genteel and nineteenth century; the most successful performance, perhaps, is that of Beatrice Straight because here a certain rigidity belongs to the character and is in any case delicately checked by the performer's fine sensibility.) The second story is that of the interpenetration of good and evil. I am afraid that Mr. Miller needs a Kazan not merely at some superficial technical level. He needs not only the craftsmanship of a Kazan but also—his sense of guilt. Innocence is, for a mere human being, and especially for an artist, insufficient baggage. When we say that Mr. Kazan "added" to *Death of a Salesman*, we mean—if I am not saying more than I know—that he infused into this drama of social forces the pressure of what Freud called "the family romance," the pressure of guilt.[2] *The Crucible* is *about* guilt yet nowhere in it is there any *sense* of guilt because the author and director have joined forces to dissociate themselves and their hero from evil. This is the theatre of two Dr. Jekylls. Mr. Miller and Mr. Kazan were Dr. Jekyll and Mr. Hyde.

NOTES

1. Since these words were written, it has been urged that Mr. Miller's hero is shown not to be faultless in that he has committed adultery. A fault indeed by seventeenth-century standards, adultery in the context of Mr. Miller's play is but a weakness, that is to say, a "fault" which author and audience forgive him—for the good reason that they're aren't sure it is a fault: it is an endearing bit of weakness. Some months after the opening reviewed above, Mr. Miller personally redirected the play in such a way as to minimize

its politics and maximize the personal story of husband, wife, and girl friend. If his intention was to prove his play not to be about McCarthyism, he failed. If any part of my original review would not apply to the later production, it is the phrase NOWHERE IS THERE ANY SENSE OF GUILT. When E.G. Marshall and Maureen Stapleton played the husband and wife, one had the sense of another impulse seeking—if not quite finding—utterance. Is it perhaps an impulse that will find utterance in another play— on the subject of the tensions of unhappy marriage?

2. [In another review also published in the collection *The Dramatic Event*, Mr. Bentley observed that Kazan's influence on the plays' productions made him virtually co-author of Miller's *Death of a Salesman* and Tennessee Williams' *A Streetcar Named Desire*, which comment had the following repercussions, as Bentley notes:] This brought me a friendly but firm note from Mr. Kazan, stating that he had not written one line either of *Streetcar* or *Salesman*. I take it Mr. Kazan includes under the heading of authorship only the dialogue. But it seems to me that if a director helps to create the very idea of a character—changing it from what it was in the author's original script—he is co-author—even though the creating and changing has been done without recourse to new dialogue. Dialogue after all is only one of a playwright's means of communication. . . .

I received a letter from Mr. Tennessee Williams' lawyer threatening legal proceedings if *The Dramatic Event* were not withdrawn from the bookstores and the offending paragraph deleted. The legal adviser of Horizon Press (my then publisher) demurred. No copies were withdrawn. No words were deleted. Then Mr. Tennessee Williams' lawyer turned out to be Mr. Arthur Miller's lawyer too. By coincidence Mr. Miller also wanted the book immediately withdrawn from the bookstores, pending the deletion of a certain paragraph. No copies were withdrawn. No words were deleted. Instead, a letter from Mr. Williams and Mr. Miller appeared in Bert McCord's column in *The New York Herald Tribune*. It ended with the words: "Mr. Bentley's statement is a lie."

In relation to my analysis of Mr. Miller's daring (now reprinted in *The Theatre of Commitment*, p. 38), the sequel is full of interest. A radio station asked Mr. Miller to discuss my book with me on the air. He said he would do so if he could bring a friend along. The friend would be Mr. Williams. But then Mr. Miller inspected a copy of *The Dramatic Event*. It seems that, at the time when he demanded the suppression of the book, he had not read it; a fact full of interest for the student of mid-century liberalism. When Mr. Miller finally did read the book, he refused to discuss it publicly, and set down his reasons in a letter marked Not For Publication. The broadcast took place. Mr. Williams and Mr. Miller were absent, but the paragraph concerning virtual co-authorship was duly transmitted to the attendant millions, and I replied to the implied arraignment with an admirably accurate paraphrase of the note above.

Mr. Kazan was asked to sign the Williams-Miller note but refused. Miss Molly Day Thacher (Mrs. Kazan) gave *The Dramatic Event* a favorable review in *The New Leader*. Mr. Williams was reported in the New York press as saying that, without Mr. Kazan, his new play, *Cat on a Hot Tin Roof*, would not have been a hit.

Interpreting *The Crucible* in a Theatrical Production

N. Joseph Calarco

While producing a performance of *The Crucible* director N. Joseph Calarco explains in the following article that his production, rehearsals, and staging revealed the power and depth of the play. In rehearsals Calarco told the actors to remember two premises: Evil is a function of will rather than an error of reason, and witchcraft was real. According to Calarco, these premises fueled uncontrollable fear as the motivating force of the play. Ironically, Calarco's task as director paralleled the role of the character Deputy Governor Danforth—both were working to reveal evil.

N. Joseph Calarco teaches theater at Wayne State University in Detroit and directs productions of the Hilberry Repertory Theatre. He is the author of *Tragic Being: Apollo and Dionysus in Western Drama.*

Theatrical production can be seen as a critical process leading to conclusions whose validity is tested before an audience. Composed of conscious insights and intuitive leaps, subject to frequent transformation during the rehearsal period, this process resists easy formulation by director, designer, and actor; when it is discussed, the perspective is typically that of an outside observer at rehearsals. What I will attempt to describe here—from a director's viewpoint—is the critical process in a production of Arthur Miller's *The Crucible* which played for two seasons in Wayne State University's Hilberry Repertory Theatre. . . .

THE DIRECTOR'S REHEARSAL PREMISE

I introduced the cast to the Puritan notion of the link between individual and community evil, quoting from Edmund S. Morgan's *The Puritan Family:* "Since the whole group had promised

Reprinted from "Production as Criticism: Miller's *The Crucible*," by N. Joseph Calarco, *Educational Theatre Journal*, vol. 29, no. 3 (1977), pp. 354–61, by permission of The Johns Hopkins University Press. Copyright © 1977 by The Johns Hopkins University Press.

obedience to God, the whole group would suffer from the sins of any delinquent member. . . . By publicly punishing him the group testified to their disapproval of his actions and so escaped responsibility for them. Incessant vigilance, however, was essential in order to prevent any sin from going unpunished. It was as if a district occupied by a military force were given notice that for any disorder the whole community would be penalized, innocent and guilty alike." Within the framework of Puritanism, something was rotten in Salem, and searching it out was a social and religious imperative.

I then announced that a major premise of rehearsals would be the reality of witchcraft—evil as a function of will rather than an error of reason—in the world of the play. The working spine of the production (subject to change as our knowledge of the script grew) would be to find the witch, as the spine of a production of *Oedipus* might be to find the murderer of Laius. We were embarking on a witch hunt.

In proposing this approach to the cast, I acknowledged that it would have two immediate, potentially dangerous effects: it would legitimize the judges' inquiry, and it would allow us to regard John and Elizabeth Proctor as being mistaken from the start. An actor noted the connection between the closed circle in which we sat and the magic circle of witchcraft. "Are we exorcising the Devil or evoking him?" "I'm not yet sure; I know only that in either case he must be revealed. But Miller's Salem seems to be the Devil's territory; let's discover its laws." The first read-through began quietly, with unusual intensity.

The practical effects of that initial discussion were immediate. Actors playing characters opposed to the witch hunt began to find the elements of doubt in their positions; actors playing judges and supporters of the witch hunt sought motivation in the imperatives of the Puritan world-view rather than simple self-interest and personal vengeance—they felt their characters were serving God, and consequently pursued the enemies of the hunt without remorse. Only Reverend Hale, seeing Antichrist in the courtroom, would reverse his position before the last act.

FEAR AS A SOURCE FOR CHARACTERIZATION

As rehearsals continued, it became clear that our strategy fueled the play's engines of uncontrollable fear. If evil is real and has manifested itself, the only possible debate is about its source. The responsibility for individual sin is universal; to deny its universality is in Puritan terms a sin. The common sense of characters like Proctor, Giles Corey, and Rebecca Nurse is an insistence on the illusion of a rational order amid the reality of chaos; that common sense is therefore sinful: it is also structurally *hamartia,* a tragic error.

Our strategy demanded that the characters be of their time and place, Puritans in a Puritan community. It has been argued (by [American playwright and drama critic] Herbert Blau among others) that John Proctor is an eighteenth-century rationalist in a seventeenth-century society, and this has been advanced as a criticism of the play. In the last act, Proctor *does* move beyond the Puritan world-view, but he begins a Puritan. If he does not attend church, it is because he despises Reverend Parris's ostentatious and ungodly greed. Proctor's sense of personal sin is so intense that the public revelation of his relationship with Abigail is made in deep shame. Proctor's scruples are in many ways stronger than those of the spiritual leaders of his community. When he is tempted by Danforth to sign his name to a lie, his eventual refusal is also a rejection of the Father of Lies and an affirmation of his link with the best members of the sacred community. If Proctor enjoys simple worldly things, they do not make him an eighteenth-century rationalist. As Morgan observes, "contrary to popular impression the Puritan was no ascetic. . . . He never praised hair shirts or dry crusts. He liked good food, good drink, and homey comforts; and while he laughed at mosquitoes, he found it a real hardship to drink water when the beer gave out." We encountered no difficulty in treating Proctor as a true Puritan in a Puritan world. . . .

As rehearsals proceeded, I realized that my role as director bore remarkable resemblances to that of Deputy Governor Danforth. Just as Danforth established court outside the courtroom, it was my task to marshal all human and scenic elements at my disposal for the purpose of revealing evil. Like Danforth, I yearned for the flight of a terrible yellow bird. We were establishing the stages of a ritual intended to exorcise the Devil, but destined to evoke him. It became increasingly clear that Act 3, the trial scene, was the formal focus of the production, the center of our magic circle, and that Danforth would emerge as the witch hunter turned witch, whose will transforms a ritual of justice into a ritual of evil. At this stage, it was impossible to say how Act 4 would work in the context of our original rehearsal strategy. If the spine of the production was to find the witch, and if he had been found in Act 3, what was left for the last act to reveal? Was it merely, as some critics have claimed, an extended denouement? We blocked it, aware that the nominal form of a trial continued, with Proctor, Elizabeth, and Hale as their own accusers, admitting to faults which did not concern the judges. In this act Satan was the Tempter, offering earthly life for a signature inscribed in the blood of falsehood, pursuing his will through the tormented Hale as well as the implacable Danforth. The logic of action and character would propel us through the last act, but its meaning in the context of the total play did not emerge until an audience entered the theatre. The opening night audience, "members of a gallery witnessing a fixed trial," completed the theatrical form of the play and provided me with a basis for articulating the critical results of the design and rehearsal strategies.

THE THEATRICAL POWER OF THE PLAY

If *The Crucible* is viewed as a well-made play, the purpose of the first act is to supply exposition and initiate the complication. However, Miller calls his first act "An Overture"; and although an overture in opera precedes dramatic action, it also contains the principal themes and may be regarded as a complete statement in itself. In performance, Act 1 proceeded at fever pitch, propelled by the immediate crisis of Betty's condition. Layers of fear and guilt emerged from the performances, moving inevitably towards the final explosion of confessions by Tituba and the children. Is this intensity, I wondered as I watched the show, excessive—establishing a level beyond which the play could not move? As a director, I knew that a production must normally pace intensities and withhold climaxes until the proper moment in the plot. The opening scene succeeded as an isolated piece of theatre, but would it give us nowhere to go? I remembered Arthur Miller's comment on *Death of a Salesman:* "What we wanted . . . was not a mounting line of tension . . . but a bloc, a single chord presented as such at the outset, within which all the strains and melodies would already be contained." But this was a different play, a different form, and it would have to stand on its own terms.

The second act began quietly, but with a tension which gradually emerged with increasing force in the dialogue between Proctor and Elizabeth, building layers of complexity with each entrance of a new character, as if all of Salem's guilt and rage were gradually filling Proctor's house. It paralleled the first act in this rising curve of intensity, but the ending was bleak, not ecstatic, building tensions rather than releasing them. Proctor and Mary Warren were alone in a corner of the stage amid shadows, the sounds of "God's icy wind" penetrating the house. The single intermission was taken at this point. The audience members were hushed in the lobby and returned early to their seats.

As the trial scene began, it was obvious that the audience was deeply involved in the proceedings. The reviews would later confirm what I observed—a stratum of tense silence which was explosively interrupted when the petulant Parris was told to sit down, when Danforth called for the arrest of the signatories to Proctor's petition, and when Danforth locked wills with Abigail. The rehearsal strategy of our production—and I believe the logic of the play—demanded that Danforth deal more savagely with Abigail than with any other witness, creating an atmosphere in which Proctor's denunciation of her, rather than comprising an isolated personal event, is an outgrowth of what has come before.

The stage was now set—quite literally—for the entrance of Elizabeth. The sequence which followed was one of those events which call our attention to the difference between literary and theatrical form. The script tells us that Elizabeth enters, and we read a dialogue between her and Danforth in which he inquires about Abigail's behavior as her servant, finally asking the question whose answer will determine whether Proctor lied when he called Abigail a whore. She answers falsely.

Theatrically, the sequence is larger and more complex. Danforth has placed Proctor and Abigail at corners of the room, facing away from Elizabeth. When she enters, her attention is locked on her husband, whose face she cannot see. "Look at me only, not your husband," says Danforth, "in my eyes only." As the line of questioning develops, Danforth repeatedly insists, "Look at me! Look at me!" Elizabeth's focus on Danforth is a thing achieved in conflict; on the stage, it was as if lines of magnetic force were pulling her towards Proctor and Abigail, lines of force held in check only by Danforth's insistent will. He is, after all, only searching for the facts, the literal facts. Finally, he puts the question to her; but he does not ask if Abigail is a whore: "Is your husband a lecher?" There is a void. Then, faintly, "No, sir."

At this point on opening night, I heard a remarkable sound—a synchronized, sharp intake of breath by an audience of over six hundred people. It seemed for a moment as if the auditorium had been emptied of air, and when it filled again it was poisonous, and chaos had come. Perhaps most remarkable would be the predictability of this event in performance after performance, a measured thing like the timing of a laugh line in comedy. Yet it became increasingly obvious, as I observed the production for two seasons and with different casts, that the preceding page of dialogue was not enough in itself to create this response, however skillfully played; and the event did not release tension like a laugh, but compounded it.

What we had found with the collaboration of the audience was the connection between the two strategic territories of production—the courtroom and the magic circle of witchcraft—and the previous action had prepared us for their tumultuous marriage.

If each scene seems formally "closed" rather than merely part of the pattern of a well-made play, it is because each is a completed trial. The first act focuses on the trial of Tituba by Parris and Hale. In Act 2, Elizabeth brings Proctor to trial; he protests that "It is like a courtroom when I come into this house." Then Proctor tries Mary Warren, who points an accusing finger at Elizabeth; Hale interrogates Elizabeth and Proctor, and Cheever finds and presents evidence of Elizabeth's guilt. In Act 3, court is convened in the anteroom of the courthouse—emphasizing the ease with which any scenic territory may be converted to that purpose—and all are on trial. The last act finds Proctor bringing himself to trial, passing through personal guilt to an accusation directed against the judges. Theatrically, each trial is complete; we do not need to see Tituba repeat her confession in court, or hear Cheever's testimony against Elizabeth again.

THE IMPACT OF THE COURTROOM SCENE

If the "courtroom" scene has a special importance, it is because it calls into question the relation of the form of a trial to the idea of justice. The point is that, formally, this is not a "bad" trial, a simple miscarriage of justice. That would be too easy an appraisal and would fail to explain Danforth's relentless attack on Abigail, the court's principal witness. Every trial depends on truthful testimony; without it, any system of justice would collapse. During the course of the play, the audience has formed opinions—based as much on passion as reason—about the difference between false and true testimony.

The play has cast the audience as the gallery—a jury without a vote engaged in a judicial process. That jury has been given every reason to believe that Elizabeth Proctor will not give false testimony, even when the truth involves a risk to her life. When she is summoned to the court, it is to give formal testimony—to declare a private truth with public consequences. Danforth posits the question: "Is your husband a lecher?" It is *judicially* a perfectly reasonable question. But Danforth is asking about more than Proctor's actions at a particular point in time; he is asking Elizabeth whether her husband may be defined as a lecher, bound irrevocably to Abigail by a single action. Elizabeth delivers true testimony about her husband (and the integrity of their marriage), testimony which is nevertheless a judicial falsehood. These are, I believe, the complexities surrounding this moment of truth, the fuse which lights an explosion in the audience.

When judicial truth becomes a personal lie, the link between social and sacred justice collapses. The trial becomes an empty form open to chaos, an exorcism of good rather than an exorcism of evil, and the judge becomes a witch. The play reverses the process achieved in the *Eumenides;* justice destroys man and unleashes the Furies. Even Proctor's confession—his true testimony—has been merely a stage in a daemonic ritual, and he acknowledges its function when he at last cries out, "A fire, a fire is burning! I hear the boot of Lucifer, I see his filthy face! And it is my face, and yours, Danforth!" Satan has been evoked, and fills the courtroom-turned-coven with his presence.

When truth has lost its potency as a defense against evil, the social and sacred justice of Puritanism cease to exist. What Proctor finally does in the last scene is internalize justice, making it a function of the relation of man to himself rather than the relation of man to social and religious abstractions. When justice is lodged in the individual, the courtroom collapses, and the polity of man and God must find a new foundation. Proctor does not reach his decision to destroy the confession through reason or faith—reason has failed him already, faith in Puritan justice was his downfall— but through a visceral rejection of the lie and through the affirmation of the value of his name, which becomes the sign of his humanity, of all flaws, perfections, and passions which cannot be reduced to testimony or signed away in blood.

In this final scene, Proctor moves beyond the Puritan cosmology, establishing a new human territory in which free will and the power of the individual to take effective action are operative realities. He does this from within, rather than as an eighteenth-century rationalist visiting a Puritan world; and his transformation occurs at a point where the Puritan community has already collapsed in a heap of dead bodies and (as we see in Reverend Hale) splintered values. The triumph of Satan in Salem is finally the death of God, but without God Satan loses his cause for being. At the end of the play, the judges are weary and broken with victory, and Danforth shrinks to the dimensions of a common hangman. In Sophocles' *Oedipus at Colonus* Oedipus rejects the terrible burden of guilt he had embraced in the previous play, and *ascends* to his death; Proctor also ascends beyond guilt to a liberating death, leaving the ashes of a theocracy behind him. He has his goodness now.

Here then is an interpretation of *The Crucible* achieved through the complete process of theatrical production— from initial study of the script through performance with an audience. The strategies chosen for design and rehearsal were critical strategies; together they led the inquiry through preliminary concepts and tentative insights to a formulation of the meaning of the play. I have engaged in criticism both outside and within the theatre, and now feel that the advantage of the latter approach is that its validity is tested in action at every moment of a performance. Out of that crucible, Miller's play yields surprising substance.

Chronology

1914–1918
World War I

1915
Arthur Miller is born in New York City, the second of three children of Isidore and Augusta Barnett Miller; Arthur has an older brother, Kermit, and a younger sister, Joan, will be born in 1921

1917–1920
Russian Revolution

1921
Miller's sister, Joan born

1928
Isidore Miller's business fails and the Miller family moves to Brooklyn

1929
The New York stock market crash and the start of the Great Depression

1933
Arthur graduates from high school to a number of odd jobs; while working as a shipping clerk, he discovers literature, including the influential Russian novel *The Brothers Karamazov* by Fyodor Dostoyevsky; President Franklin D. Roosevelt introduces New Deal reforms

1934
Miller enrolls at the University of Michigan

1936
Miller's first play, *No Villain*, wins University of Michigan's Avery Hopwood Award for drama

1937

Miller's play *They Too Arise*, a revised version of *No Villain*, earns a prize from the Theatre Guild Bureau of New Plays and his *Honors at Dawn* wins Avery Hopwood Award

1938

Miller graduates with a degree in English; moves back to New York and writes scripts for the Federal Theatre Project

1939–1945

World War II and the Holocaust

1940

Miller marries his college sweetheart, Mary Grace Slattery

1941

Japan bombs Pearl Harbor, December 7

1944

Miller's first child, Jane, is born; Miller tours army camps and writes a book of military reportage, *Situation Normal.* His first drama to play on Broadway, *The Man Who Had All the Luck*, closes after only six performances

1945

Miller's novel *Focus* is published; first atomic bomb is dropped on Hiroshima; Japanese surrender ends WWII in the Pacific

1947

Miller's second child, Robert, is born; after many drafts, Miller's play *All My Sons* is produced; 328 performances later, the play wins the New York Drama Critics Circle Award

1949

Death of a Salesman opens in New York City; wins the Pulitzer Prize and the Antoinette Perry Award; Miller also publishes "Tragedy and the Common Man," the first of many essays on the nature of drama

1950–1953

Korean War

1950

Miller meets actress Marilyn Monroe; he writes an adaptation of Henrik Ibsen's play *An Enemy of the People*; McCarthyism and the Red Scare take hold in Washington

1953

The Crucible opens on Broadway

1955

Miller begins a relationship with Marilyn Monroe; writes *A View from the Bridge* and *A Memory of Two Mondays*

1956

Miller divorces Mary Slattery and marries Marilyn Monroe; he is subpoenaed to appear before the House Un-American Activities Committee (HUAC) and is cited for contempt of Congress; *A View from the Bridge* opens in London

1957

Miller's short story "The Misfits" appears in *Esquire* magazine; Miller also publishes *Collected Plays*; Soviet Union launches *Sputnik*, the first man-made satellite

1958

Miller's HUAC contempt conviction is reversed

1961

Miller's screenplay *The Misfits* is filmed starring Marilyn Monroe; Monroe and Miller divorce

1962

Miller marries photographer Inge Morath; Marilyn Monroe commits suicide; Cuban missile crisis

1963

President John Kennedy is assassinated in Dallas

1964

After the Fall opens in January and *Incident at Vichy* premieres in December; President Lyndon Johnson commits U.S. soldiers to the conflict in Vietnam

1965

Miller is elected president of the International Association of Poets, Playwrights, Editors, Essayists, and Novelists

1967

Miller publishes a collection of short stories, *I Don't Need You Anymore*

1968

The Price opens on Broadway; *Death of a Salesman* reaches sales of one million; Martin Luther King Jr. is assassinated in Memphis

1969

America lands a man on the moon

1970

Miller's works are banned in the Soviet Union as a result of his work to free dissident writers

1971

The Portable Arthur Miller is published

1972

The Creation of the World and Other Business opens and closes after twenty performances; Watergate scandal begins with burglary at Democratic Party national headquarters in Washington, D.C.

1974

Richard Nixon resigns U.S. presidency

1975

Miller works to free convicted murderer Peter Reilly; the last Americans are evacuated from Vietnam

1977

Miller petitions the Czech government to halt arrests of dissident writers; writes *The Archbishop's Ceiling*

1980

The American Clock premieres

1982

Miller writes two one-act plays, *Elegy for a Lady* and *Some Kind of Love*; Vietnam War memorial is unveiled in Washington, D.C.

1983

Miller and his wife travel to China to see a production of *Death of a Salesman* in Beijing

1984

Dustin Hoffman plays Willy Loman in a Broadway revival of *Death of a Salesman*; Ronald Reagan is elected to a second term as president

1985

Death of a Salesman airs on television to an audience of twenty-five million

1986

Miller writes *Danger: Memory!*

1987

Miller's autobiography, *Timebends: A Life,* is published

1990

Miller writes a screenplay for the motion picture *Everybody Wins*; President George Bush launches Operation Desert Storm against Iraq

1991

Miller's play *The Ride Down Mt. Morgan* opens in London; dissolution of the Soviet Union

1993

Miller's comedy-drama *The Last Yankee* premieres in New York

FOR FURTHER RESEARCH

BIOGRAPHICAL WORKS AND INTERVIEWS WITH THE PLAYWRIGHT

Bernard Dekle, "Arthur Miller," *Profiles of Modern American Authors.* Rutland, VT: Tuttle, 1969, pp. 147–53.

Richard I. Evans, *Psychology and Arthur Miller.* New York: E.P. Dutton, 1969.

Bruce Glassman, *Arthur Miller.* Englewood Cliffs, NJ: Silver Burdett, 1990.

Jean Gould, "Arthur Miller," *Modern American Playwrights.* New York: Dodd, Mead, 1966, pp. 247–63.

John Gruen, "Arthur Miller," *Close-Up.* New York: Viking, 1968.

Elia Kazan, *Elia Kazan: A Life.* New York: Knopf, 1988.

Arthur Miller, *Timebends: A Life.* New York: Grove, 1987.

Benjamin Nelson, *Arthur Miller: Portrait of a Playwright.* New York: David McKay, 1970.

Matthew C. Roudané, ed., *Conversations with Arthur Miller.* Jackson: University Press of Mississippi, 1987.

ABOUT *THE CRUCIBLE* AND MILLER'S PLAYS

Harold Bloom, ed., *Modern Critical Views: Arthur Miller.* New York: Chelsea House, 1987.

Neil Carson, *Arthur Miller.* New York: Grove, 1982.

Harold Clurman, *Lies Like Truth.* New York: Simon & Schuster, 1958.

Robert Corrigan, ed., *Twentieth Century Views: Arthur Miller.* Englewood Cliffs, NJ: Prentice-Hall, 1969.

John H. Ferres, ed., *Twentieth Century Interpretations of* The Crucible. Englewood Cliffs, NJ: Prentice-Hall, 1992.

Ronald Hayman, *Arthur Miller.* New York: Ungar, 1972.

Sheila Huftel, *Arthur Miller: The Burning Glass.* New York: Citadel, 1965.

Robert A. Martin, ed., *Arthur Miller: New Perspectives.* Englewood Cliffs, NJ: Prentice-Hall, 1982.

Walter J. Merserve, ed., *The Merrill Studies in* Death of a Salesman. Columbus, OH: Charles E. Merrill, 1972.

Leonard Moss, *Arthur Miller.* Rev. ed. Boston: Twayne, 1980.

Brenda Murphy, *Miller:* Death of a Salesman. Cambridge, England: Cambridge University Press, 1995.

Benjamin Nelson, *Arthur Miller: Portrait of a Playwright.* London: Petrowen, 1970.

Gerald Weales, *American Drama Since World War II.* New York: Harcourt, Brace & World, 1962.

Sidney Howard White, *The Merrill Guide to Arthur Miller.* Columbus, OH: Charles E. Merrill, 1970.

HISTORICAL BACKGROUND

Thomas Adler, *American Drama, 1940–1960: A Critical History.* New York: Twayne, 1994.

Gerald M. Berkowitz, *American Drama of the Twentieth Century.* London: Longman, 1992.

C.W.E. Bigsby, *Modern American Drama, 1945–1990.* Cambridge, England: Cambridge University Press, 1992.

Kenneth C. Davis, *Don't Know Much About History.* New York: Avon, 1990.

David Halberstam, *The Fifties.* New York: Fawcett Columbine, 1993.

Frederick Lumley, *Trends in 20th Century Drama.* New York: Oxford University Press, 1960.

George Jean Nathan, *Theatre in the Fifties.* New York: Knopf, 1953.

G.J. Watson, *Drama: An Introduction.* New York: St. Martin's, 1983.

WORKS BY ARTHUR MILLER

Arthur Miller's works are available in a wide variety of anthologies and reissues; therefore, facts of publication are omitted from the following list. All works are plays unless otherwise noted.

No Villain (1936)

Situation Normal (journal); *The Man Who Had All the Luck* (1944)

Focus (novel) (1945)

All My Sons (1947)

Death of a Salesman (1949)

Adaptation of Henrik Ibsen's *An Enemy of the People* (1950)

The Crucible (1953)

A View from the Bridge; *A Memory of Two Mondays* (1955)

Collected Plays (1957)

The Misfits (the screenplay) (1961)

After the Fall; *Incident at Vichy* (1964)

I Don't Need You Anymore (short stories) (1967)

The Price (1968)

The Creation of the World and Other Business (1972)

The Archbishop's Ceiling (1977)

The American Clock (1980)

Elegy for a Lady; *Some Kind of Love* (1982)

Danger: Memory! (1986)

Timebends: A Life (autobiography) (1987)

The Ride Down Mt. Morgan (1991)

The Last Yankee (1993)

INDEX